BEYOND ALL WORDS

Hymn Texts 2003 – 2011
by
Alan Gaunt

*To David
with all good wishes
Alan*

Stainer & Bell

First published in 2011 by
Stainer & Bell Limited, PO Box 110, Victoria House, 23 Gruneisen Road,
London N3 1DZ, England.

All rights reserved. This book is copyright under the Berne Convention.
It is fully protected by the British Copyright, Designs and Patents Act 1988.
No part of the work may be reproduced, stored in a retrieval system, or
transmitted in any form by any means, electronic, photocopying or otherwise
without the prior permission of Stainer & Bell Ltd unless otherwise stated below.

The copyright in the compilation, prefatory material, notes, typography and
music setting of this volume vests in Stainer & Bell Ltd.

The music to No. 39 is within the public domain.

Material reproduced by permission of third parties is acknowledged on the page
concerned and full details are given on pages 116–117. Every effort has been made to trace
all owners of copyright; if any have unwittingly remained undiscovered, the publishers
offer apologies and will gladly make full acknowledgement in any future edition.

The copyright in the individual music (including musical arrangements) of all hymns
(except No. 39) and the copyright in the individual hymn texts vests in Stainer & Bell Ltd.
For permission to reproduce any text or tune owned by Stainer & Bell Ltd, application
should be made to Hope Publishing Company, 380 South Main Place, Carol Stream,
Illinois 60188 for the USA and Canada and Stainer & Bell Ltd for all other territories.

Local Copying
The texts of Alan Gaunt may also as at the date of publication be copied by those holding
a current Church Copyright Licensing Ltd licence provided the items copied are included
on their returns.

The cover image is by Alan Gaunt and is used by kind permission.

British Library Cataloguing-in-Publication Data
A catalogue record of this book is available from the British Library

Catalogue No. B923

ISBN 978 0 85249 923 8

Printed in Great Britain by Caligraving Ltd, Thetford

This becomes the axis on which the whole hymn turns, leading back to the theme of creation and renewal. In this collection the hymn which sums up that movement with the same kind of drama is one about the incarnation – 'Eternal God, you live and move / in light too bright for human sight'. The first verse is essentially an affirmation, followed then by two verses in narrative form; the conclusion is

> And from that darkest place on earth,
> your light has poured across the years;
> faith, hope and love are brought to birth,
> and joy springs up through grief and tears.
> Love stoops to conquer earth's despair;
> we reach the cross and find you there. (62)

So Alan returns to the central truths of Christian faith, the completed work of Christ in cross and resurrection, which in turn lead to the Trinitarian understanding of God as one in three persons. Whether read as meditations or sung as congregational celebrations, there is much in this collection to appeal to young and old, wise and simple. The contents deserve to become widely known, and it is a privilege to commend them.

DAVID M. THOMPSON May 2011
Emeritus Professor of Modern Church History,
University of Cambridge

Author's Preface

Beyond All Words: this title comes from the last line of No. 6 in the collection: a text which stresses that all human anguish is shared by God. It begins, 'When no words can suffice / to tell the hurt we feel' and ends, '... all who are distressed / will find the promise true / in joy, here unexpressed, / beyond all words, with you.'

In 2002, I received a letter from a friend in which he told me that another friend of his had said that the longer he lived, the less he believed. I can understand that. The longer I live, the more distressed I become about the horrific things that happen in the world, and I can well understand how housebound elderly people, watching all the bad news on television, become depressed. I do not think that I believe less, except in the sense of putting away a certain shallow optimism, but I find that, more and more I have to put my faith in Dietrich Bonhoeffer's statement, 'Only a suffering God can help.'[4] William Temple said, 'Only a God in whose perfect Being pain has its place can win and hold our worship, for otherwise the creature would in fortitude surpass the Creator.'[5] And the reality of that is the God who is *beyond all words*.

> A rumbling: it is
> Truth itself
> walked among
> men,
> amidst the
> metaphor squall.[6]

It is probably true that all the most important statements we make as human beings, whether in science or faith, are part of that 'metaphor squall'. Can anything we say of God be factual? We can only speak metaphorically about God; nothing we can say about God is actual *fact*. It may be that all the most serious divisions between Christians arise from the *fact* that we think that all that we say about God is *fact*. But to say that what we believe about God is not *fact* does not mean that it is, therefore, untrue. On the contrary it can be said that *myth* is truer than *fact*. Truth *really* does walk among us 'amidst the metaphor squall.'

When we have said all that we can about God, there is still more to be said: the meaning of God's power and love, as proclaimed by the prophets, as we have seen it in Jesus Christ, and experienced it through the Holy Spirit, is always *beyond all words*. But through prayer, the reading of the

---

[4] *Letters and Papers from Prison* (Fontana Books, 4th impression, 1963; first published in English by SCM Press, 1963), p.122.
[5] *Readings in St John's Gospel, Second Series* (Macmillan, 1940), p.385.
[6] *14 Poems from Breathturn*, from *Selected Poems and Prose of Paul Celan*, translated by John Felstiner (Norton, 2001), p.277.

Scriptures and other forms of worship, and also the singing of hymns, we can come closer and enter more fully into the experience of God's reality which, thank God, really is *beyond all words*!

I wrote a sonnet along these lines, *Never Understood*. It begins, 'That was the day when you first came to me ...' The sestet says:

> My brain was stormed by every word I heard,
> my mind relentlessly weighed down, and yet
> my heart was riding smoothly like a bird
> on truth's wild thermals! I do not forget
> the joy that day when I received all good
> and knew: it never could be understood.[7]

However, these hymns have been written in the hope that when they are sung or read, the singers or readers may realise, or rediscover, something of the truths of God, which storm the brain, but lift the heart 'on truth's wild thermals', keeping hope and joy alive, and faith going forward, precisely because they are *beyond all words*!

ALAN GAUNT

May 2011

---

[7] *The Space Between* (Songster, 2009), p.22.

Hymn Texts
in chronological order

*With thanks
to Winifred, to our family
and to all
whose loving encouragement
through the years
has been beyond all words*

1 What ails my child

LOVE SONG

What ails my child,
what does he see?
At first he smiled,
but then he gazed at me
with grief-filled eyes
as though his birth
had made him wise
to all the pain on earth.

And suddenly
my mother-joy
has frightened me,
has made me lift my boy
and hold him here
against my breast,
to still my fear
and set my heart at rest.

He is asleep
and I am calm.
I will not weep,
but keep him safe from harm
until he grows
away from me,
and then who knows
just what my son will be.

My sheer delight
in him runs deep.
Not darkest night,
nor death itself will keep
the love we bear
in grief for long;
so I still dare
to sing my joyful song.

© Copyright 2001 Stainer & Bell Ltd

Written 22 August 2001

Metre: 4.4.4.6.D.

Suggested Tune: SCOTFORTH

Author's Note: Written for a Christmas card.

SCOTFORTH

Jenny Canham (1947–)
Arranged Alison Hale (1969–)

1 What ails my child, what does he see? At first he smiled, but then he gazed at me with grief-filled eyes as though his birth had made him wise to all the pain on earth.

2 And sing my joyful song.

© Copyright 2011 Stainer & Bell Ltd

2 My child sleeps quietly

My child sleeps quietly
held safely on my breast;
the night came silently
and we are both at rest.
We rest, we are not scared,
we find the dark no threat;
my child and I have shared
no grief or terror yet.

And yet I have a dream:
a sword goes through my heart;
I hear young mothers scream,
their children torn apart.
Then as the nightmare clears
I wake to dawning light;
with eyes still streaming tears,
I hold my own child tight.

Is there no mother-love
to drown such dreams as this,
no love to rise above
earth's hate and prejudice?
I wake from troubled sleep,
where war and crime run wild,
I yearn for love too deep
to lose a single child.

I learn through my child's birth
the depth of love I share,
which pleads for peace on earth
in every mother's prayer;
and if bad dreams combine
with grim reality,
this love more sure than mine
holds tight eternally.

© Copyright 2003 Stainer & Bell Ltd

Written 2 April 2003

Metre: 6.6.6.6.D.

Suggested Tune: COLLIERY GREEN

Author's Note: Written for a Christmas card, 2004. Dedicated to Ali Ismaeel Abbas and all the innocents mutilated by war.

COLLIERY GREEN

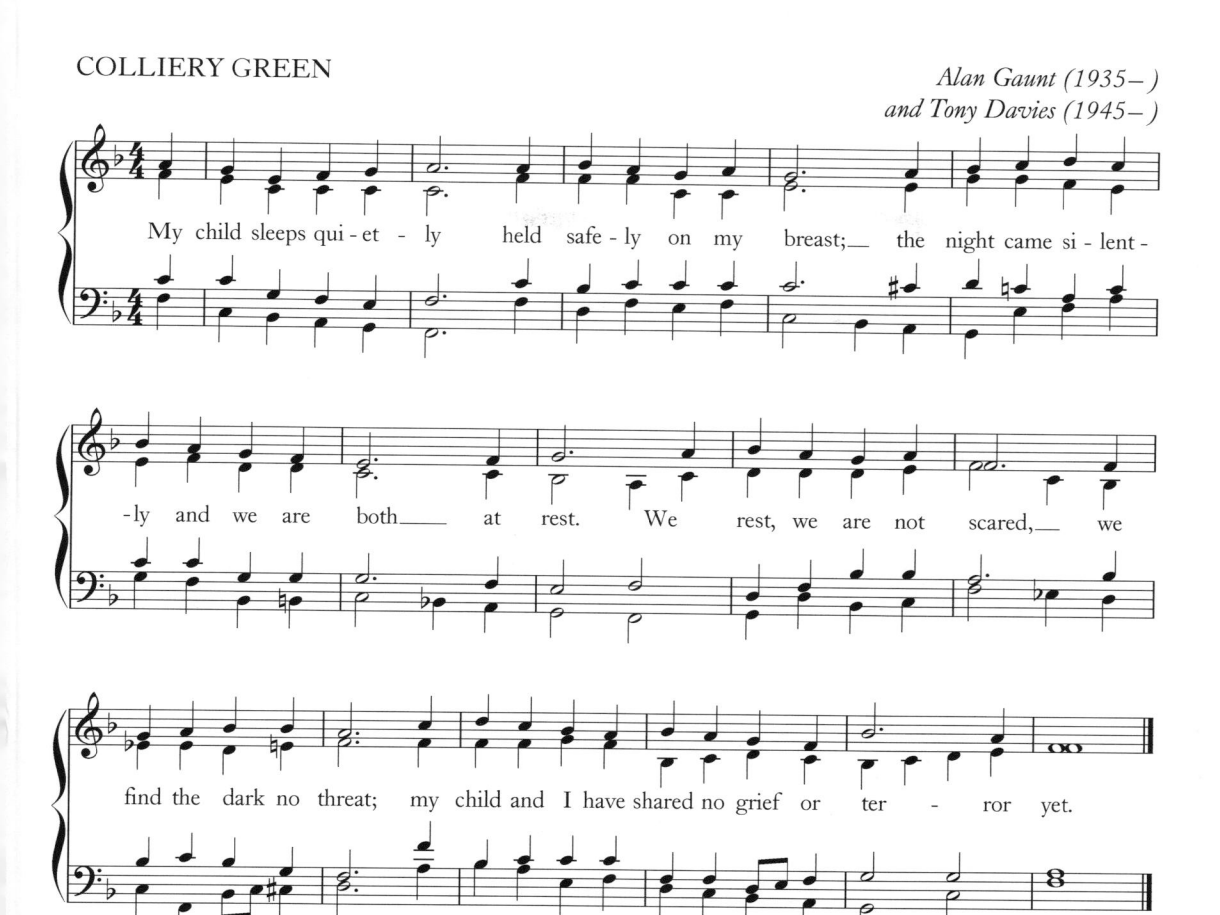

Alan Gaunt (1935–)
and Tony Davies (1945–)

My child sleeps quietly held safely on my breast; the night came silently and we are both at rest. We rest, we are not scared, we find the dark no threat; my child and I have shared no grief or terror yet.

© Copyright 2011 Stainer & Bell Ltd

3 We praise your dying love

In loving memory of Thomas Caryl Micklem, 1925–2003

We praise your dying love,
dear Christ, because with you
through life and death we rise above
the worst the world can do.

Through all life's pain and loss,
though we may grieve and weep,
the joy which led you to the cross
still flows as sure and deep.

Its living fountains rise
from love's eternity:
delight, to take us by surprise
in all adversity.

When life might seem too long,
through wearying distress,
refreshing springs will keep us strong
to cross the wilderness.

And when life seems too short,
our loved ones' years too few,
we trust, with them we shall be brought
to deathless joy with you.

Through all our future days,
still keep our faith secure,
until in fullest joy we praise
your love for ever sure.

© Copyright 2003 Stainer & Bell Ltd

Written 10 June 2003

Metre: SM

Suggested Tune: DUNDRENNAN

Author's Note: Ever since I first sang it, I have loved Caryl Micklem's tune to Isaac Watts's 'My soul repeat his praise', which brings out of that paraphrase a much greater depth of meaning and meditative feeling than the more familiar, four-square GILDAS. In seeking to honour Caryl's memory, and to speak to his family, DUNDRENNAN was the tune that immediately came to mind.

4 Great crucified and risen Lord

Great crucified and risen Lord,
supreme in love's true artistry,
give us the grace, in joy or grief,
to live our lives creatively.

Give us a heart like yours, to grasp
love's self-effacing righteousness,
with moral force to demonstrate
the power of wounded holiness.

Give us the art in this harsh world,
where rage and violence run wild,
to be the makers of your peace:
each truly named, with you, God's child.

Love's great creative artist, form
God's image in us, more like you,
and by your Holy Spirit draw
love's healing art from all we do.

© Copyright 2003 Stainer & Bell Ltd

Written 13 August 2003

Metre: LM

Suggested Tune: HAWKHURST

Author's Note: This text was originally written to follow a dramatic reading of the Beatitudes in an act of worship celebrating creativity. It was subsequently considerably revised, moving away from direct reference to the Beatitudes, though they remain at the root of it.

5 John the Baptist told King Herod

BABYLON
Alan Gaunt (1935–)

© Copyright 1997 Stainer & Bell Ltd

John the Baptist told King Herod, 'Just watch what you do!
Don't you know the holy God has got his eyes on you?
Yes, God has you in his gaze,
and if you don't mend your ways,
you will soon discover bad behaviour never pays!'

Now King Herod was a weak and rather foolish king,
one who wanted his own way in almost everything,
but he liked to hear John preach
though perplexed by what he'd teach,
because John reached parts that other preachers could not reach.

But he had him flung in prison, just to illustrate
that as king he might go further and decapitate
any cheeky underling
who might stand up questioning
the deportment and behaviour of a noble king.

Herod's birthday gave his wife an opportunity,
at a party for the rich and great of Galilee:
for she really hated John
and her hatred drove her on
and she'd never rest content till he was dead and gone!

So her daughter danced for Herod and the drunken king
was delighted, saying, 'You can have just anything!
Yes, a gift however great,
up to half of my estate,'
so she chose the head of John the Baptist on a plate.

Then the king was most upset, but he had made his vow
and, as all his guests had heard him, couldn't draw back now;
so he called his guards and said,
'Go and get the Baptist's head,'
so they brought it on a plate and John was truly dead.

So the king, his wife and daughter, in their infamy,
have gone down, discredited and shamed, in history;
whereas John the Baptist's fame
still remains a living flame,
and still makes us brave to serve the Gospel we proclaim.

© Copyright 2003 Stainer & Bell Ltd

Written 2 July 2003

Metre: 13 13.7 7 13.

Suggested Tune: BABYLON

Author's Note: An all-age song, linked to the Gospel reading for 16 July 2003, which was *Mark* 6:14–29.

6 When no words can suffice

For Mary Wheatley

When no words can suffice
to tell the hurt we feel,
and kindly meant advice
is powerless to heal;
Christ of Gethsemane,
though we have no relief,
once anguished there, you see
and share our deepest grief.

When shallow words we say,
said with no depth of care,
just push their pain away
that neighbours need to share;
then Christ of Calvary,
forsaken and alone,
you know their agony
and bear it as your own.

When words have all been said,
and silence takes its hold,
when emptiness and dread
take over, dark and cold;
Christ, bring us through the night
and show us at its heart,
the rapturous delight
God promised from the start.

Though human pain persists,
and many know despair,
yet childlike faith insists
Love answers anguished prayer;
and all who are distressed
will find the promise true
in joy, here unexpressed,
beyond all words, with you.

© Copyright 2003 Stainer & Bell Ltd

Written 9 July 2003

Metre: 6.6.6.6.D.

Suggested Tune: BEYOND ALL WORDS

Author's Note: I spoke on the phone to our friend, Mary, suffering from apparently uncontrollable cancer: a fact which she accepted calmly, though not without sorrow. We communicated by email, and I felt that my spoken and written words were completely inadequate. I then wrote her a poem beginning 'Words Being Not Enough ...'

The hymn came out of the poem. Mary died on 1 October 2004.

BEYOND ALL WORDS

Alan Gaunt (1935–)
and Tony Davies (1945–)

When no words can suf-fice to tell the hurt we feel, and
kind-ly meant ad-vice is pow-er-less to heal; Christ
of Geth-se-ma-ne, though we have no re-lief, once
an-guished there, you see and share our deep-est grief.

© Copyright 2011 Stainer & Bell Ltd

7 Forgive us, God, each crass attempt

Forgive us, God, each crass attempt
to seek our own aggrandisement;
forgive the smugness and contempt
that disregards the innocent.

Forgive our self-made confidence,
our self-advancing self-esteem,
our self-deceit, which lacks the sense
to thrust aside self's futile dream.

Forgive us when we dare to tread
roughshod across defencelessness,
or resolutely seek to spread
our bias as your righteousness.

Forgive us when we crucify
your love, and blatantly abuse
your holy name, to justify
the evil means we dare to use.

Forgive us, God, and take away
faith-counterfeiting faithlessness;
break through our unbelief, display
in us your truth and tenderness.

Then by our passion for your will,
reflecting Christ's humility,
God, challenge those who hate and kill,
to turn and heal earth's enmity.

© Copyright 2003 Stainer & Bell Ltd

Written 8 October 2003

Metre: LM

Suggested Tune: HERONGATE

Author's Note: I wrote a poem called *The Ultimate Amendment*, which gave ironic expression to my feelings about the commercial *imperialism* of the United States. It began, 'Rebuild the towers to point for ever up / to our aggrandisement ...' I knew, of course, that the will to self-made aggrandisement was not confined to the United States, and that even the Church was by no means free of it: or myself for that matter. Hence, these words, which are not directed at the United States!

8   You will not fail us, great God our Creator

You will not fail us, great God our Creator,
through all life's dangers your Spirit is here;
your mighty love that has suffered in Jesus,
comes, resurrected, to banish our fear.
This is our confidence: in Christ love died for us;
we are his people, we live to proclaim
through love that dares to die evil is conquered;
we face life's dangers with joy, in his name.

Christians before us have trusted and suffered,
facing the threat of defeat and death's loss,
but, with your Spirit, have conquered their terror,
choosing, with Jesus, to take up their cross.
Chorus

So in these days, with your poor still tormented,
broken by war and oppressed by despair,
pierce our false peace with the power of your Spirit,
conquer our selfishness: God, make us care!
Chorus

Now let us live to serve you in our neighbours
and, though life's dangers still make us afraid,
in Jesus crucified, bleeding and helpless,
we see love's greatness supremely displayed.
Chorus

© Copyright 2003 Stainer & Bell Ltd

Written 21 October 2003

Metre: 11.10.11.10. and Chorus 12.10.11.10.

Suggested Tune: FAITHFULNESS

Author's Note: Written to the tune FAITHFULNESS. People who love to sing this tune will probably want to stay with its familiar words. I have to confess that I find those words just a bit too reassuring and unchallenging, and all for ME. I felt moved to compose words that still expressed Christian assurance, but made it, perhaps, more challenging.

9 Dancing Holy Trinity

Dancing Holy Trinity,
holy and profound,
perfect mutuality,
ever freely bound:
from your flawless harmony
thrilling notes resound;
filled with your divinity
this earth is holy ground.

God, as blazing stars stampede
through expanding space,
faith still dares, in them, to read
your unmeasured grace:
dancing on with timeless speed
and unwearied pace,
till the dance, as love decreed,
includes the human race.

Jesus, you were born to wear
human flesh and show
God's great love, and so to bear
grief as cold as snow.
Now your music fills the air
and, with you, we know
how to dance God's joy and share
your love with friend and foe.

Holy Spirit, you invite
us to dance with you;
so direct our steps aright,
keep our timing true.
Living Flame of love ignite
our cold hearts, renew
joy and hope, and let love's light
shine out in all we do.

Dancing Holy Trinity,
dance through all our days;
with love's choreography
startle and amaze;
coming from eternity
set our souls ablaze
so that faith's community
fills all the world with praise.

© Copyright 2003 Stainer & Bell Ltd

Written 27 October 2003

Metre: 7.5.7.5.7.5.7.6.

Suggested Tune: PARSLEY HAY

Author's Note: Reading Colin E. Gunton's *The One, The Three and the Many: God, Creation and the Culture of Modernity* (Cambridge University Press, 1993), I wanted to take up the theme of *perichoresis* (literally, *going round*, *rotation* or *circumincession*, used of the reciprocal existence of the persons of the Trinity). Not originally, I wanted to express it as the eternal dance of the Three in One. Community in God creates community in creation.

PARSLEY HAY   *Matthew Redfearn (1963–)*

Dancing Holy Trinity, holy and profound,
perfect mutuality, ever freely bound:
from your flawless harmony thrilling notes resound;
filled with your divinity this earth is holy ground.

© Copyright 2011 Stainer & Bell Ltd

10   Eternal Spirit, once you drove

Eternal Spirit, once you drove
your Christ into the wilderness,
and gave him strength and freedom there
to choose the way of helplessness.

And then you gave him all God's power
to enter on his ministry,
to demonstrate eternal love
in service and humility.

And, in the garden, when his heart
was broken as he faced hope's loss,
you braced his prayer and steeled his will
to stand again and meet the cross.

As he was nailed, you gave him voice
to call forgiveness down on them:
the ones who hammered home the nails,
whom tortured love would not condemn.

When he was buried in the tomb,
you still stayed close to him and spread
your love around him lying there,
divine and human, with the dead.

You waited through death's second day,
and then your deep life-giving breath
delivered him, God's child reborn,
resplendent from the void of death!

© Copyright 2004 Stainer & Bell Ltd

Written 27 October 2003 (verse 6 added 28 March 2004)

Metre: LM

Suggested Tune: EISENACH

Author's Note: Reading Colin E. Gunton's *The Promise of Trinitarian Theology* (T & T Clark International, 2003), I was struck again by the realisation that God never left the crucified Christ, but that God's Trinity of Love remained intact, as the Holy Spirit led the human Jesus all the way through birth, life, death, resurrection and ascension.

11 God, destroy the bigotry

God, destroy the bigotry
that makes faith's truth a lie;
purge us of the enmity
which forces love to die.
Come and share the agony
of those who grieve their loss,
through the same hostility
that took Christ to the cross.

Banish the hypocrisy,
the oily, smooth veneer,
sham, that makes a mockery
of all that Christ holds dear.
Give us his integrity
to keep faith true and clean,
always speaking lovingly
but saying what we mean.

Wipe away our blasphemy
that violates your name,
justifying cruelty
that still puts faith to shame.
Give us sensitivity,
to love and not disown
those whose faith and certainty
are different from our own.

Loving Holy Trinity,
defeat our bitterness,
ending insularity
and healing loneliness.
Come in loving sovereignty,
help us, on earth, to raise
your love's true community
of freedom, joy and praise.

© Copyright 2003 Stainer & Bell Ltd

Written 22 November 2003

Metre: 7.6.7.6.D.

Suggested Tune: TUNE FOR MARY (Alan Gaunt: *Delight that Never Dies*, No. 12. Stainer & Bell, 2003)

Author's Note: Paul Celan's bitter poem, translated by John Felstiner as *Late and Deep*, is a fierce and justified challenge to my Christian faith. It challenges, especially, those Christians who '... cry blasphemy!'

> We've known it long since.
> Known it long since, but who cares?
> You grind in the mills of death the white meal of the promise ...
> ...
>
> You warn us: Blasphemy!
> We know it full well,
> let the guilt come on us ...'
>
> (from *Selected Poems and Prose of Paul Celan*, translated by John Felstiner. Norton, 2001)

But on whom does the guilt come? Surely, on all those bigots, of Christian or any other faith, who accuse others of blasphemy, refuse them love, or hold on to attitudes that lead to persecution, bloodshed and war.

12 Any child born to loving parents

Any child born to loving parents might
transform their lives with wonder and delight.
Innocence stakes its overwhelming claim,
drawing its life from love's persistent flame.

Helplessness reigns and, in an infant's cries,
innocence schools the wisdom of the wise;
Infancy, with relentless guileless art,
claims the complete devotion of the heart.

When this harsh world with all its cruelty
makes parents weep, lamenting bitterly,
innocence slain, though silenced, loudly cries,
its claim still heard and heeded by the wise.

So, once again we celebrate Christ's birth,
greeting his love that risked its life on earth.
This is the time to come with confidence,
greeting in him our own first innocence.

© Copyright 2004 Stainer & Bell Ltd

Written 3 January 2004

Metre: 10 10.10 10.

Suggested Tune: MAGDA

Author's Note: The birth of Christ as a helpless innocent, and the massacre of the innocents by Herod, reminds us of the duty owed to all helpless innocents by all humanity, in the family, the community and the state. And if that duty is ever to be ultimately fulfilled, it requires that we all become 'like little children' – innocently wise.

13 Christ, from eternity

For Ruth Micklem and family

Christ, from eternity,
appearing like a bird,
through your divine fragility
Love's voice was heard.

Eternal Love took wing
on earth and soared in you;
for those who listened to you sing
Love's song rang true.

At last you soared so high
that Love's heart-piercing song
filled all the air, to testify
against earth's wrong.

But fowlers closed their ears,
they brought you to the ground;
and, by their loud discordant jeers,
Love's song was drowned.

And then on Calvary
they nailed you up to die:
God's lovebird plucked ingloriously,
love made a lie!

But from your final breath,
true love's integrity
came homing through the gales of death,
triumphantly!

© Copyright 2004 Stainer & Bell Ltd

Written 23 February 2004

Metre: 6.6.8.4.

Suggested Tune: CORROUR BOTHY

Author's Note: This was completed on what would have been my brother's 72nd birthday. I was working through Stella Aldwinckle's long poem, or series of poems, *Christ's Shadow in Plato's Cave* (The Amate Press, 1990). This text was sparked by lines from two poems:

> Here in my hand now
> The wounded bird
> Lies still in death
> Homed out of pain
> To the Heart of God.

(*Death as Perfection*, from Stella Aldwinckle: *Christ's Shadow in Plato's Cave*. The Amate Press, 1990)

and

> In this one place of GOD'S ONE WORD
> Seen Homing Thro' Golgotha's Death
> Back to the HEART OF GOD.

(*God's Love*, from Stella Aldwinckle: *Christ's Shadow in Plato's Cave*. The Amate Press, 1990)

I was also thinking about some of Caryl Micklem's simple flowing tunes, and the text came to fit CORROUR BOTHY.

14 Loud, from the cross, a shout is heard

Loud, from the cross, a shout is heard,
and all earth's pain is in that cry.
All life seems futile, Love absurd,
when Love's voice bellows, 'My God, why?'

In Love's cry here, all nature pleads
for meaning in earth's pain and fear;
each living thing that hurts and bleeds
protests in Love's voice dying here.

Here earth's Creator wears its pain,
enrobed in human helplessness;
in flesh, God cannot bear the strain
and cries to God in hopelessness.

But where Christ hangs without a friend,
broken, with nails in hands and feet,
there love proves faithful to the end
and triumphs in its own defeat.

All human and all creatures' cries
are gathered into that one cry,
and everything that lives and dies
will share the answer to Love's 'Why?'

Here faith discerns God's mystery,
and glimpses every creature's worth,
here Mother-Love bears history
towards creation's final birth.

© Copyright 2004 Stainer & Bell Ltd

Written 24 February 2004

Metre: LM

Suggested Tune: BRESLAU

Author's Note: In *Christ's Shadow in Plato's Cave*, Stella Aldwinckle writes, under the title *God's Sacrament*, of

>The Cloak of God's Own Pain
>In each and every creature's
>Pain and death Embody'd
>
>For each one's borrow'd life,
>Out of pain and death is now
>Seen as ever being Form'd
>And Shap'd and Perfected
>For Creation's Final Birth
>Back into God ...

In the next poem, *God's Footfall*, she writes

>All Men's cries
>And all dumb creature's cries
>Are in the One Great Cry
>Of Dereliction Summ'd ...
>
>(from Stella Aldwinckle: *Christ's Shadow in Plato's Cave*. The Amate Press, 1990)

It is in Vernon Watkins's poem, *Deposition, On the Painting by Ceri Richards*, that he writes

>Love has for triumph
>Its own defeat.
>
>(*The Collected Poems of Vernon Watkins*. Golgonooza Press, 1986)

15   Jesus, uniquely bodied in each neighbour

Jesus, uniquely bodied in each neighbour,
each human person is your sacrament,
through whose delight or sorrow you still labour
to breach the walls of our imprisonment.

When love of self deludes us and enslaves us,
you come to meet us in our neighbours' need,
and in their presence your compassion saves us:
in them we meet you, to be bound and freed.

When neighbours faced by hatred and destruction
suffer and bleed and see their loved ones die,
your voice, though silently, repeats the question,
which from your cross still rends us: 'Why, God, why?'

In those whose love, worked out in deeds of kindness,
rebukes our pride with true humility,
you are among us, come to heal the blindness
of faithless prejudice and bigotry.

Your body, broken once for all, still broken
in all who suffer, still calls us to prayer;
the blood in human veins remains the token
of your life lost, found here for all to share.

© Copyright 2004 Stainer & Bell Ltd

Written 12 March 2004

Metre: 11.10.11.10.

Suggested Tune: INTERCESSOR

Author's Note: Stella Aldwinkle, in her poem *God's One Body*, says,

> Human body is God's sacrament supreme ...
> Explaining quite exactly
> Why bad acts are bad
> and good acts good ...

She also writes

> Of God uniquely Body'd in my neighbour
> Uniquely suffering here and now.

(from Stella Aldwinckle: *Christ's Shadow in Plato's Cave*. The Amate Press, 1990)

16 Speak to us, Christ, in strangers

Speak to us, Christ, in strangers,
the truth you would impart,
lest the closed mind endangers
the wholeness of our heart.

Those whose beliefs offend us,
rejected out of hand,
may be the ones you send us
to make us understand.

You speak in those neglected
and those we castigate;
you come, quite unexpected,
in enemies we hate.

In those who criticise us,
and fault our narrow ways,
speak sternly to surprise us,
set searing love ablaze.

Save us from moral blindness
and give us ears to hear,
in others' loving kindness,
your voice, dispelling fear.

Then we will trust more surely
your love, once crucified,
and greet and share, more truly,
your joy, from far and wide.

© Copyright 2004 Stainer & Bell Ltd

Written 13 March 2004

Metre: 7.6.7.6.

Suggested Tune: CHRISTUS DER IST MEIN LEBEN

Author's Note: Thomas Merton said, 'God must be allowed to speak unpredictably. The Holy Spirit, the very voice of Divine Liberty, must always be like the wind in "blowing where he pleases" (John 3:8) ... We must find him in our enemy, or we may lose him in our friend. We must find him in the pagan or we will lose him in our own selves ...' (*A Letter to Pablo Antonio Cuadra Concerning Giants* from *The Collected Poems of Thomas Merton*. New Directions Publishing Corporation, 1977.)

17 God, speak to us in all who meet us

God, speak to us in all who meet us:
through fierce and mild unfold your grace;
reveal yourself in human features:
the angry look, the smiling face.

When we are faced with accusation,
in other people's rage or grief,
let us not shun your condemnation
of our self-love and unbelief.

From our self-righteousness deliver
the ones we judge too easily:
the sinner and the unbeliever,
who mirror our own frailty.

When we receive your loving kindness
from those with whom we disagree,
show us that you have come to find us
in their angelic ministry.

Then give us faith's imagination
to fathom Love's theology,
and in unlooked for revelation
to see and praise Love's Trinity.

© Copyright 2004 Stainer & Bell Ltd

Written 14 March 2004

Metre: 9.8.9.8.

Suggested Tunes: SPIRITUS VITAE and LES COMMANDEMENS DE DIEU

Author's Note: Thomas Merton said, 'It is my belief that we should not be too sure of having found Christ in ourselves until we have found him also in the part of humanity that is most remote from our own.' (*A Letter to Pablo Antonio Cuadra Concerning Giants* from *The Collected Poems of Thomas Merton*. New Directions Publishing Corporation, 1977.)

18 As Christ hangs crucified

As Christ hangs crucified
and true love bleeds,
his arms are stretched out wide,
as though he pleads
for pity and release
from agony,
to share again, in peace,
Love's Trinity.

His friends in disbelief,
have seen him nailed
and, in their fear and grief,
think love has failed.
His outstretched arms seem now
to question why
such grief should be, or how
such love could die.

Observe the cross and see
what God will do,
who bears earth's cruelty
for love of you:
whose arms are opened here
to draw us out
from numbing sorrow, fear,
despair and doubt.

We turn our loving gaze
on Christ who died
and all our lives we'll praise
the Crucified;
for through his death we face
eternity,
and in his arms embrace
Love's Trinity.

© Copyright 2004 Stainer & Bell Ltd

Written 20 March 2004

Metre: 6.4.6.4.D.

Suggested Tune: CLIFF TOWN

Author's Note: One of Stella Aldwinckle's poems is entitled *Christ's Lifted Arms*, which are 'upstretched' ...

>Pointing us Up, Out of Death
>Into the Life of God ...

In another poem, *Flesh Transfigured*, she writes of 'Calvary's Arms of Three-Person'd Love' ...

>Ever Reaching His and our
>Three-Person'd Birth Up Into
>The Life and Rest of God.

>(from Stella Aldwinckle: *Christ's Shadow in Plato's Cave*. The Amate Press, 1990)

19 There is no limit, God

There is no limit, God,
to what your love will do,
or just how far your love will go
to meet us, in our need.

Not only have you worn
our dying flesh, but you
have bowed yourself to undergo
derision and disdain.

When Jesus was on trial
you were a prisoner, there;
and when he heaved his cross you were
too weak with pain and fell.

Hanged high on Calvary,
and faced with love's defeat,
you cried against earth's rage and hate
in his cry, 'My God, why?'

As love itself decreed,
with hope and promise lost,
you lay there, null and void, and passed
your Sabbath with the dead.

And so you made your case
against power's stubborn lie:
your love at death's extremity,
still points earth's way to peace.

© Copyright 2004 Stainer & Bell Ltd

Written 29 March 2004

Metre: SM

Suggested Tune: WINDERMERE

Author's Note: This takes up again Alan E. Lewis's *shocking* theme of God, present in Christ, without divine protection, so that we 'have heard the astounding news that love as self-surrender is the truth for us, because it is first the truth of God's own life and being.' (*Between Cross and Resurrection: A Theology of Holy Saturday* (Eerdmans, 2001), p.99.) The wilfully imperfect rhyme may, perhaps, be taken as symbolic of love's willing defeat!

20   There was a day

There was a day
when Love lay dead;
all hope, all joy
and promise bled
into the ground;
and, through the dark and dread,
God uttered not a sound!

Disciples numbed,	There come such times
beyond relief,	when evil thrives,
had never plumbed	and hell, its crimes
such depths of grief,	let loose, deprives
or ever known	the earth of light,
such total disbelief,	consigning wasted lives
with spirits turned to stone.	to silent, loveless night.

Then those who trust
must stand and bear
hell's stifling dust
that fills the air;
not brush away
the heart's despair, but dare
to grieve till Love's third day.

© Copyright 2004 Stainer & Bell Ltd

Written 27 March 2004

Metre: 4.4.4.4.4.6.6.

Suggested Tune: GRIEF

Author's Note: Before his death from cancer, Alan E. Lewis was able to finish his book, *Between Cross and Resurrection: A Theology of Holy Saturday* (Eerdmans, 2001). He wrote there: 'The day that follows it [Saturday] is not an in between day which simply waits for the morrow, but it is an empty void, a nothing, shapeless, meaningless and anti-climactic, simply the day after the end.' (p.31). Many ministers, and others, regret the fact that so many Christians miss out Good Friday from their worship and meditation, so that Easter Day tends to be trivialised, losing its truly amazing quality, as the gift of God's Grace, coming out of grief, despair and total loss: the grief, despair and total loss that still happen, and which faith must face.

GRIEF

Gwilym Beechey (1938–)

dolce ed espressivo, **p** - **mp**

There was a day when Love lay dead; all hope, all joy and prom-ise bled in-to the ground; and, through the dark and dread, God ut-tered not a sound!

© Copyright 2011 Stainer & Bell Ltd

21 Christ, nations, hard at war

Christ, nations, hard at war,
blind in their ruthlessness,
make killing normal and ignore
your pleas for gentleness.

When will love banish hate?
When will humility,
refusing to retaliate,
extinguish enmity?

As lust for power deceives
and fear and hate increase,
deluded politics believes
new wars will win us peace.

Christ, show yourself in those
who suffer and must bear
contempt and anguish, in the throes
of terror and despair.

As vengeance still runs wild,
let us not justify
the violent death of any child:
Christ, let us rather die!

Yes, break our hearts, remove
all coldness and disdain;
let your compassion in us prove
your love, that bears earth's pain.

Christ, give us faith today
to trust you, crucified;
against all odds you took God's way
and triumphed as you died.

© Copyright 2004 Stainer & Bell Ltd

Written 31 March 2004

Metre: SM

Suggested Tune: SOUTHWELL

Author's Note: In Christ, God endured human violence and went through suffering and death, for love of the whole human race. Christ still comes to us in the victims of war, and goes on giving his one simple answer: there is no hope of peace, except by the way of humble, un-retaliating love between all human beings and, ultimately, between all nations. This is the logic of the Gospel we proclaim.

22 Christ, challenge us to understand

Christ, challenge us to understand
your going to the Cross:
not clever tactics neatly planned,
but hideous total loss.

Refusing to retaliate
or pay back cruelty,
you offered only love for hate,
and perished helplessly.

Your resurrection is the sign
that love outlives all wrong,
but does not make success divine
or sanctify the strong.

We mar the Gospel we proclaim,
and make your truth a lie,
by seeking triumph in your name,
while helpless victims die.

There is no true security
in threat and counter threat;
no peace, when faced with enmity,
in giving what we get.

For only love that dares to die
and share the cross with you,
can nullify hate's deadly lie
and prove the Gospel true.

Let risky, daring faith increase
and help us pay love's price,
to show God's only way to peace
through love's self-sacrifice.

© Copyright 2004 Stainer & Bell Ltd

Written 4 April 2004

Metre: CM

Suggested Tune: HARINGTON

Author's Note: 'Love's power is actually powerless to impede huge triumphs of ... evil ... in the world.' So said Alan E. Lewis. He then went on to suggest that it is 'only through vulnerable victimisation' that 'the Triune God of righteous love' can flourish. (*Between Cross and Resurrection: A Theology of Holy Saturday* (Eerdmans, 2001), p.261.) Only by learning, from Christ, and following the way of God's vulnerable love, can Christians ever hope to stem the overwhelming tide of evil versus evil, attack and counter-attack, war and retaliation.

23 Suffering servant

Suffering servant,
keep us aware,
ever observant
of the anguish you bear:
you are still sharing
sorrow and pain
and your love, unsparing,
in victims of hate is still slain.

Hatred keeps driving
love from the heart;
prejudice, thriving,
forces people apart;
ignorance loudly
passes on blame,
and flaunts itself proudly,
presuming to speak in your name.

Do not forsake us,
stay at our side;
come and remake us,
undermine all our pride.
Make your Church holy,
loving like you,
as humble and truly
self-giving in all that we do.

In all earth's wildness,
warfare and strife,
give us your mildness,
truest strength of our life.
Where people suffer
pain and despair
there let us offer
your healing, the fruit of our prayer.

In all life's bleakness,
trusting your word;
hindered by weakness
when our hope seems absurd,
faith out of fashion,
scorned or ignored;
sustain our compassion
still serving your world, servant Lord.

© Copyright 2004 Stainer & Bell Ltd

Written 6 April 2004

Metre: 5.4.5.6.5.4.6.8.

Suggested Tune: SERVANT LORD

Author's Note: Another struggling response to the challenging reality of Alan E. Lewis's *Between Cross and Resurrection: A Theology of Easter Saturday* (Eerdmans, 2001).

SERVANT LORD

Gwilym Beechey (1938–)

Andante teneramente

Suf-fer-ing ser-vant, keep us a-ware, ev-er ob-ser-vant of the an-guish you bear: you are still shar-ing sor-row and pain and your love, un-spar-ing, in vic-tims of hate is still slain.

© Copyright 2011 Stainer & Bell Ltd

24   The darkest day was past

The darkest day was past,
new morning came at last;
the numbing grief of loss gave way
to stunning joy that day.
The death-defeating Word
had died, but now was heard
proclaiming Love's great victory,
fought out on Calvary.

The dark and silent tomb
became the living womb;
the Mother-Spirit gave new birth
to Love, which filled the earth.
As hopelessness took flight,
new wonder and delight
broke out to greet, through doubt and dread,
the First Born from the dead.

Then, with expectancy,
the new community
received its life with Christ who died,
no longer terrified;
the peace that he bequeathed,
the Spirit that he breathed,
inspired prophetic eloquence
and daring confidence.

Though we are still afraid
and constantly dismayed,
by all earth's unrelieved distress
and our own feebleness;
inspire us, Living Word,
and let God's truth be heard.
Through our weak words and deeds, express
Love's powerful powerlessness.

© Copyright 2004 Stainer & Bell Ltd

Written 6 April 2004

Metre: SMD

Suggested Tune: ICH HALTE TREULICH STILL

Author's Note: In his book *Between Cross and Resurrection: A Theology of Holy Saturday* (Eerdmans, 2001), Alan E. Lewis emphasises that Easter Saturday links, inseparably, Good Friday and Easter Sunday. The Resurrected Christ is the Crucified Christ. The Victorious One, whom the Church proclaims, remains the powerless One, who judges not only the world, but the Church and every Christian individual, in their will to power.

25 Lord, whose wealth is all around us

Lord, whose wealth is all around us,
though your promises astound us
and your challenges dumbfound us,
you remain as kind and true.

We go after earthly treasure,
worldly goods and passing pleasure;
but the good beyond all measure
is the wealth we have with you.

Though our feeble faith still wavers
and earth's idols still enslave us,
you stay faithful and will save us
from the false hopes we pursue.

So, Lord, when we're in a flurry,
when we rush about and scurry,
chasing riches, full of worry,
make us calm, at peace with you.

In the confidence that faith brings,
full of hope and joy, the heart sings;
you are faithful, Lord, in all things:
come and make us faithful too.

© Copyright 2004 Stainer & Bell Ltd

Written 4 August 2004

Metre: 8 8 8.7.

Suggested Tune: QUEM PASTORES

Author's Note: A response, in all-age worship, to *Matthew* 6:19, 20 and 33.

26   God, save from cruel persecution

God, save from cruel persecution
all living things, with whom we share
your miracle of evolution,
which rises up to praise and prayer.

All creatures, whether fierce or gentle,
wear fragments of your majesty,
revealing something sacramental
which points to love's eternity.

The fiercest creature in creation,
in spite of its ferocity,
cannot incur the condemnation
deserved by human cruelty.

For none but humankind, for pleasure,
can take sheer malice in its stride,
tormenting innocence for pleasure,
and hunting creatures down in pride.

And only humans, for their reasons,
treat creatures as commodities,
enslaving them in cruel conditions
regardless of their miseries.

God, in your Word made flesh, once wearing
our earthly dust, although divine,
meet us in all earth's creatures, sharing
your Spirit, as in bread and wine.

© Copyright 2004 Stainer & Bell Ltd

Written August 2004

Metre: 9.8.9.8.

Suggested Tunes: SPIRITUS VITAE and LES COMMANDEMENS DE DIEU

Author's Note: A hymn-writer should not be producing controversial texts that fellow Christians cannot sing with integrity. A hymn-writer should not be expressing his or her own views, as distinct from proper Christian convictions (though what are they?). This does not mean that one should be writing texts that all Christians can sing easily. This text, however, came out of my own feelings about the demonstrations of the Countryside Alliance, in favour of hunting with dogs. I do, and I do not, apologise. The text also owes something to Andrew Linzey's *Animal Theology* (SCM Press, 1994).

27 Jesus, our friend, you are always near

For Roger Brooks

Jesus, our friend, you are always near,
and though we wander far from you,
when we return in our need or fear,
we find you still for ever true.

Your promise stands, your integrity
will never change, your love will stay
steadfast and sure in its constancy,
our strength and comfort day by day.

No friend on earth is more sure than you,
and through all our disloyalty
your love remains still as deep and true
through time into eternity.

If we are lost, hurt and in despair,
or overwhelmed by earth's distress,
most gracious friend you will meet us there
with joy to heal our bitterness.

Jesus, our friend, make us more like you,
whose gentle kindness never ends;
and let us be ever sure and true,
your loving, firm and faithful friends.

© Copyright 2005 Stainer & Bell Ltd

Written 10 September 2004, revised 17 July 2005

Metre: 9.8.9.8.

Suggested Tunes: LOVELY JOAN and O WALY WALY

Author's Note: Roger Brooks was my friend from *c*.1942 to 1946 when, with my family, I left Blackpool. I saw him twice after that: on 8 September 1950 and in September or October 1953, when I called for him and we went to a football match together. We did not meet or communicate again until 2003. On that occasion Roger showed me a letter which I had written for his birthday (1946 or 1947), in which I had promised lifelong friendship. A promise that may, after all, be fulfilled.

28 Here, in this world of sadness

Here, in this world of sadness,
where God in Christ has shared our sorrow,
leap up for joy and gladness,
and make Love's promise known.

Though grief and pain, persisting,
breed anguish and distress,
God's love which gave us Jesus
brings joy from hopelessness.
Chorus

Though war, brute force and terror
kill hope and stifle prayer,
God's judgement, rich with mercy,
still brings hope from despair.
Chorus

Go to the world, proclaim it,
let God's just will be done,
till joy and gladness flourish
with Love's great triumph won.
Chorus

© Copyright 2004 Stainer & Bell Ltd

Written 6 October 2004

Metre: 7.6.7.6. and Chorus 7.9.7.6.

Suggested Tune: GO TELL IT ON THE MOUNTAIN

Author's Note: This is an attempt to express, in a simple way, faith's conviction that in spite of all the world's evil and pain (and even *through* them) joy and love will ultimately overcome. Meanwhile we will go on proclaiming this *simple* conviction.

29   Here, God is present with us

Here, God is present with us,
who meets us in this place;
and Christ who died comes, risen,
with overflowing grace.

Here, God is present with us,
and blessing is assured;
through every threat and danger,
our future is secured.

The Spirit, present with us,
still brings the Church to birth:
and calls us, as God's children,
to serve and bless the earth.

Here, God is present with us,
whose healing everywhere,
through every pain and sorrow,
protects us from despair.

Yes, God is present with us,
through all our changing days,
Creator, Christ and Spirit,
our source of joy and praise.

© Copyright 2004 Stainer & Bell Ltd

Written 17 November 2004

Metre: 7.6.7.6.

Suggested Tune: EDMONDSHAM

Author's Note: Written for an act of worship with the laying on of hands.

30 See where the birds

For Kay Andrews, the artist, and all involved in the making of the panels at Parkgate and Neston United Reformed Church

See where the birds
are winging to the skies,
like rising prayers
and soaring songs of praise.
The hills, like faith,
stand sure beneath their flight,
the water shines
with joy's reflected light.

The art and craft
of human minds and hands
give space and hope,
in which the soul expands
and finds fresh ways
to value and translate
life's brimming joys,
for faith to celebrate.

And over all,
within and all around,
God's Spirit breathes,
and every sight and sound
proclaims God's love
that has, and will, enfold
all things that live,
and never lose its hold.

Yet sometimes dread
mars every sound and sight,
when cruelty
and hatred hide love's light:
as when love died
in Jesus on the cross,
and hope despaired,
confronting total loss.

But through it all,
Love's radiance reappears,
the cross itself
illuminates our fears;
the Spirit's joy,
beyond the reach of words,
empowers our prayer
and praise, to soar like birds.

© Copyright 2004 Stainer & Bell Ltd

Written 10 November 2004

Metre: 4.6.4.6.D.

Suggested Tune: DISTANT HILLS

Author's Note: The worship area at Parkgate and Neston United Reformed Church underwent considerable redevelopment in 2004, and at Pentecost 2005 a set of large panels was dedicated which depicted the hills of Wales across the Dee estuary, with flocks of rising birds. The panels were designed by Kay Andrews and twenty-six people spent a thousand hours completing them. This text, written in advance, seemed appropriate to the panels and to the day.

DISTANT HILLS

Tony Davies (1945–)

See where the birds are wing-ing to the skies, like ris-ing prayers and soar-ing songs of praise. The hills, like faith, stand sure be-neath their flight, the wa-ter shines with joy's re-flect-ed light. birds.

© Copyright 2011 Stainer & Bell Ltd

31 Eternal God, whose love is ever true

A HYMN AFTER SUDDEN DEATH

*For Dorothy
in loving memory of Frank*

Eternal God, whose love is ever true,
though frail faith falters in the face of grief;
when hurt hearts find it hard to trust in you,
in your compassion, help our unbelief.

When, without warning, death comes suddenly,
numbing our hearts with piercing loneliness,
where can we turn, in grief's perplexity,
to rediscover hope in our distress?

You have been always there for us, in those
whose loss in death makes us so cruelly sad.
In our bereavement, faced with sudden close,
show us love's deeper depths and make us glad.

Assure us that the love which we have shared
is not diminished by our grievous loss;
show us how love continues, unimpaired,
in Christ who lived for love and bore the cross.

Through all the pain and tears we have to face,
held in the love that death cannot destroy;
with broken hearts, secure in love's embrace,
we search grief's depths for resurrecting joy.

© Copyright 2005 Stainer & Bell Ltd

Written 24 January 2005

Metre: 10.10.10.10.

Suggested Tunes: ELLERS and EVENTIDE (Monk)

Author's Note: Frank Baylis, an old friend, was one of the men who flew in unarmed reconnaissance Mosquitoes over Germany in World War II. Aged 82, he had been in the best of health and full of enthusiasm for many aspects of life, including the secretaryship of his local United Reformed Church. He was hit and killed when crossing the road. After attending his packed funeral service, I felt compelled to write – something. It was sung later at his memorial service.

32 With Jesus as our mirror

With Jesus as our mirror,
we look with open eyes,
to see ourselves more clearly,
removing all disguise.
Sometimes we look with horror,
and wish the mirror lied.
It shows us too severely
the blemishes we hide.

But when we look more deeply
a miracle takes place;
we poor and blushing creatures
see our transfigured face;
and with our latent beauty
enhanced and undefiled,
we recognise the features
of God's own precious child.

Then with delight, and eager
to see and recognise
the shining light of Jesus
in every neighbour's eyes,
we love and serve each other
and pray our love will show,
till everyone who sees us
shares in love's overflow.

God, make our faith a mirror
where neighbours see their face
enhanced in Christ-like glory,
transfigured by your grace;
and bring the nations nearer
to that tremendous day
when love completes faith's story
and drives all fear away.

© Copyright 2005 Stainer & Bell Ltd

Written 3 February 2005

Metre: 7.6.7.6.D.

Suggested Tune: AURELIA

Author's Note: In the *Odes of Solomon* 13 we read

> See! The Lord is our mirror:
> open your eyes,
> look into it,
> learn what your faces are like.
>
> (*The Odes and Psalms of Solomon* by J. R. Harris and A. Mingana, 2 vols. Manchester University Press and Longmans, Green, 1916–1920)

What are we really like? If what we saw in the mirror were our true self – the self we are deep inside – how would we look to ourselves? We might be horrified! But, if we were to see ourselves reflected back by the crucified and risen Christ, we would recognise ourselves, each one God's beautiful child: in the words of Henry Francis Lyte, 'ransomed, healed, restored, forgiven'. And we would look lovingly for the image of Christ in every neighbour, sharing love, looking towards love's ultimate reconciliation of all creation.

33 When helpless infants suffer pain

For Sylvia Lyon

When helpless infants suffer pain,
and parents watch their children die,
how can we, God, still trust in you
and not in anger ask you, 'Why?'

When faced with parents, in their loss,
so deeply wounded, numbed by grief,
how dare we cheapen costly love
with easy talk about belief?

What faith have we to share with them
when we ourselves are mystified
and ask each other, 'Where is God,
if death has won and hope has died?'

You came in Christ, an innocent;
you took upon you, at his birth,
the risk of sorrow, pain and loss,
and all the dangers of the earth.

Your love, rejected and despised,
was lifted on the cross to die.
Engulfed by grief's deep darkness there
he too, in anguish, asked you, 'Why?'

The darkness overwhelmed you there,
yet undiminished love won through.
Help us, when faced with sorrows now
to trust our helplessness to you.

Though we are silenced by the pain
that tears grief-stricken souls apart,
give us compassion, strengthen faith,
to keep and hold them in our heart.

© Copyright 2005 Stainer & Bell Ltd

Written 2 March 2005

Metre: LM

Suggested Tune: HERONGATE

Author's Note: A four-year-old child had died. People who had known and cared for her asked why God had let her die, and felt helpless in face of the parents' refusal of sympathy.

34 We have not seen you with wounded hands

We have not seen you with wounded hands;
we were not with disciples where
they rushed to hide after you had died;
we did not see you risen there.

We have not seen you as Thomas saw,
when in that room he stood, wide-eyed,
as you, so real, challenged him to feel
the wounds still in your hands and side.

He did not touch you, he had no need
to test your wounds or crudely prod;
awed with the sight, in amazed delight,
he saw and cried, 'My Lord and God!'

He did not fail you from that day on:
responding to your love's command,
he saw you there and went on to share
faith's blessing in a distant land.

We have not seen you, but we believe
you are alive with us, to be
our God and Lord, living and adored
through time and in eternity.

We have not seen you and yet we share
in your love which, once crucified,
now calls us out from our dread and doubt,
to spread faith's blessing far and wide.

© Copyright 2005 Stainer & Bell Ltd

Written 26 March 2005

Metre: 9.8.9.8.

Suggested Tunes: SEARCHING FOR LAMBS and O WALY WALY

Author's Note: This was originally written for all-age worship, when Thomas was the theme. I have always wanted to emphasise that *John* does not say that Thomas actually did touch the wounds of Jesus. He *saw* and believed. And Jesus's words to him are not a rebuke, when he says, 'Blessed are those who have not seen and yet have come to believe.' (*John* 20:29, *NRSV*). It refers to everybody in the future who, without seeing, would believe the apostolic proclamation. The fourth verse hints at the strongly held tradition of the Malabar Christians (S. W. India) that Thomas took the Gospel to India.

35 Tell all the world about it

Tell all the world about it,
proclaim the news that Christ is risen;
sing out with joy and gladness,
now Jesus lives again!

His terrified disciples
had hid themselves away,
but there he stood before them
that resurrection day.
Chorus

They'd seen him dead and buried
and they were in despair,
but now they were delighted
to see him standing there.
Chorus

He sent them as apostles
to spread the news and say
that death and sin were conquered
on resurrection day.
Chorus

So run and tell the nations,
that love will never cease
till God's work is completed
in justice, joy and peace.
Chorus

© Copyright 2005 Stainer & Bell Ltd

Written March 2005

Metre: 7.6.7.6. and Chorus 7.9.7.6.

Suggested Tune: GO TELL IT ON THE MOUNTAIN

Author's Note: Written for all-age worship for Sundays at Easter.

36 Two people walked their weary way

Two people walked their weary way,
home from Jerusalem;
the whole of life, in their dismay,
had lost its joy for them.
But as they talked so wearily,
though they were unaware
who walked with them companionably,
the Christ they mourned was there.

They told the stranger, bitterly,
how their great hope had died,
that Jesus had been cruelly
condemned and crucified.
He told them then, that suffering
was love's sure consequence,
love's only way of conquering:
its true magnificence.

Come, Jesus, walk beside us here,
upon your Easter way;
remove the joylessness and fear
of faith's dark Saturday.
Accept our invitation, be
our guest, then love, once dead,
will be alive as gloriously
as when you broke the bread.

© Copyright 2005 Stainer & Bell Ltd

Written 12 April 2005

Metre: CMD

Suggested Tune: KINGSFOLD

Author's Note: A straightforward retelling of, and response to, the story of Cleopas and the other disciple on Easter Day, *Luke* 24:13–31.

37 There is a day when faith discerns

GOOD FRIDAY
LEADS TO HOLY SATURDAY

There is a day when faith discerns
the depths of God's humility,
whose love is infinite and yearns
to heal earth's inhumanity.

We contemplate Christ on the cross
then, grieving for the life he gave,
we face God's day of total loss,
when Love lies buried in the grave.

We see faith's deepest mystery:
God's love and human hatred meet,
and at the heart of history,
Love triumphs in its own defeat.

As we face darkness and despair,
God, lead us through our unbelief;
and by your Spirit show us where
Love's joy leaps up from deepest grief.

© Copyright 2005 Stainer & Bell Ltd

Written 15 April 2005

Metre: LM

Suggested Tune: WAREHAM

Author's Note: Having already written words relating to Ceri Richards's painting, *The Deposition*, I was reading again Vernon Watkins's poem on that same painting, in which he has two lines which have haunted me:

> Love has for triumph
> Its own defeat.
>
> (*The Collected Poems of Vernon Watkins*. Golgonooza Press, 1986)

This text for Good Friday came out of that line. It also has in mind the reality that too many Christians seem to miss out Good Friday and Easter Saturday, but where else can the true meaning of Easter Sunday be discerned?

38 God, our Creator, Source of truth and justice

*For David Peel and the Wirral District
of the United Reformed Church*

God, our Creator, Source of truth and justice,
stride through earth's storms until all terrors cease;
defeat our warlike ways, our pride in battle,
brute force and cruelty that still increase:
sweep them aside in your relentless passion,
through steadfast love bring in your reign of peace.

Forbid our futile dwelling on past glories
and morbid gloom regarding present days.
Come, where our faith is spiritless and barren,
to show us living springs in desert ways:
love's endless source of deeply flowing rivers,
quenching our thirst, inspiring us to praise.

Called to repent of doubt and disillusion,
we turn again to you, Christ crucified;
now resurrected, giving us your Spirit,
with hope and joy to take life in our stride.
The promise is for us, for children's children,
and all whom God will call from far and wide.

So, God of life, and new life, keep us faithful,
renew the Church and make us worthy heirs
of the apostles, building on their teaching,
still breaking bread, in joyful hope that shares
faith's fellowship of love which, overflowing,
will bring earth peace, fulfilling all our prayers.

© Copyright 2005 Stainer & Bell Ltd

Written 5 July 2005

Metre: 11.10.11.10.11.10.

Suggested Tune: SOM STRANDEN

Author's Note: David Peel was Moderator of the United Reformed Church Assembly, 2005–6, when his theme was 'Encountering Church', based on *Isaiah* 43:15–21 and *Acts* 2:38–47. When he visited the Wirral District, I was asked to write words to be sung in one act of worship that he led.

39 Holy Spirit, gentle dove

Cornelie Booth (1864–1920)

ev - ery - where, in words and deeds all un - der-stand.

Holy Spirit, gentle dove,
God's eternal peace and love;
Pentecost gale and God's living fire,
Holy Spirit, come and inspire
our praise and service, and give us here
your love which banishes our fear.

Claim all our lives and send us out to share
the truth in Christ, obeying his command
to tell God's good news everywhere,
in words and deeds all understand.
Chorus

Claim all our actions, let love's justice guide
all that we do and everything we say,
till your truth humbles ruthless pride
and perfect love drives fear away.
Chorus

Claim all our thoughts and flood them with the light
of your deep joy which, through earth's grief, can raise
our hearts like birds in buoyant flight
to thrill the earth with joy and praise.
Chorus

© Copyright 2005 Stainer & Bell Ltd

Written 10 May 2005

Metre: 10.10.8.8. and Chorus 7 7.9 8.9 8.

Author's Note: The choir of Parkgate and Neston Church were interested in the words and music about the Holy Spirit written and composed by Mrs Herbert H. Booth, but they were not too happy about what they saw as rather old-fashioned words. I was asked to work on the words and, after producing an *anonymous* version, I revised it into its present form.

40 Stay here where nails are driven

Stay here where nails are driven
hard through Love's tender hands;
for where Love's side is riven,
faith, pierced by grief, still stands.

This is where faith discovers
the length to which Love goes;
this is where grief uncovers
the deepest truth Love knows:

The joy of faith, though dying,
springs up for ever new;
its song breaks out from crying,
and sorrow keeps it true.

So wait, where pain and grieving
engulf complacency,
in earth's despair believing
the truth of Calvary.

Then see, through desolation,
how grief and joy are tuned
to rise in exultation
because of Love's deep wound.

© Copyright 2005 Stainer & Bell Ltd

Written 11 July 2005

Metre: 7.6.7.6.

Suggested Tune: SHRUB END

Author's Note: Vernon Watkins wrote:

> Always it is from joy my music comes
> And always it is sorrow keeps it true.

(*Sonnet, To Certain Ancient Anonymous Poets*,
from *The Collected Poems of Vernon Watkins*. Golgonooza Press, 1986)

and Watkins also wrote:

> Nothing but grief could match the joy in his heart.
> The wound of love was his, the unhealing wound.

(*The Childhood of Hölderlin*,
from *The Collected Poems of Vernon Watkins*. Golgonooza Press, 1986)

Walter Brueggemann, writing about Jeremiah's sorrow and the sorrow of God, says, 'Only grief permits newness ... If God had not grieved ... there would be no newness.' Relating the theme to Christ, he says, 'In God's attentive pain, healing happens.' (*Hopeful Imagination: Prophetic Voices in Exile*. Fortress Press, 1986.) Chosen for the new Methodist hymnbook, *Singing the Faith*, published in 2011.

41 This world so full of hatred

This world so full of hatred needs
love's tireless gentle care;
where wounded, broken bodies bleed,
compassion kneels to share;
it bears the cost of bitterness
and, stooping down to feel
the pain of grief and deep distress,
it draws on love to heal.

Compassion's measure is best known
in all its healing power,
where love itself is overthrown
and faith and hope turn sour:
not in the optimistic scene,
where all seems sweet and calm,
but where revenge and hate have been
and done their greatest harm.

So dare to learn compassion there,
as once, when on the cross,
Christ cried to God in love's despair
when faced with total loss;
and there in love's despised defeat,
rejected, left to die,
God, bearing nails in hands and feet,
was pleading, 'Why, God, why?'

In God's own anguish there, discern
the cruel and bitter weight
of long-held grievances, and learn
the love that pierces hate.
To break hate's cycle, let love live
and pierce our own hearts here,
where God to God cries out, 'Forgive'
against earth's guilt and fear.

© Copyright 2005 Stainer & Bell Ltd

Written 23 July 2005

Metre: CMD

Suggested Tune: THIRD MODE MELODY

Author's Note: With the news full of suicide bombings, in London and Egypt as well as Iraq, and with the sense that violence, far from diminishing, seemed to be increasing in the twenty-first century, one felt the need to come back to the cross and reach for the depth of God's love which was given expression there. There is no other power that can pierce hatred, including our own, and bring about ultimate forgiveness and reconciliation.

42   God, give us grace to rise above

God, give us grace to rise above
the blindness of our prejudice;
teach us unsentimental love,
to grasp the healing truth we miss.

Where bitterness and hatred turn
to vengefulness that kills and maims,
help us, not guiltless, there to learn
your grace that challenges and shames.

Bring us again to Calvary, We cannot match his greatness there:
to see love helpless in death's throes, our fear of hidden enemies
and Jesus, treated ruthlessly, consumes our hope and we despair
who pleads forgiveness for his foes. of love's vast possibilities.

Give us love's mind to comprehend
the cause of passions that divide.
In us, let hatred meet its end,
as we proclaim the Christ who died.

Love, deeper than earth's deepest wrong,
drive out our fear and enmity,
fulfil the hope for which we long:
your peace for all humanity.

© Copyright 2005 Stainer & Bell Ltd

Written 25 July 2005

Metre: LM

Suggested Tune: BRESLAU

Author's Note: In face of the news of continuing violence and suicide bombings, one had to try to give expression to the reality of prejudice and enmity, not only in the minds and hearts of suicide bombers and those who encourage them to die, but also in ourselves. We, who are not without guilt, strive through love to understand the causes of violent enmity, and to overcome not by multiplying violence, but by deeper understanding of Love's sacrifice on Calvary.

43   It is too late to pray

It is too late to pray
when evil has been done;
when love is crucified
and dark clouds hide the sun;
it is too late to pray when death
has snatched away love's final breath.

It is too late to pray
when victims' anguished fears
have been proved justified;
and too late then for tears,
when tortured, work-worn, broken slaves
lie crowded in their unmarked graves.

When famine does its worst,
and parents in despair
see starving children die,
it is too late for prayer;
too late for prayer when those who should,
have failed to give the help they could.

When war and tyranny
have taken life away
and grief and terror reign,
it is too late to pray;
too late, when rulers still release
the dogs of war and murder peace.

Forgive us, God, that we
have left our prayers too late,
or missed your answering voice
that calls us to create
communities of peace and break
the chain of hate, for your love's sake.

Still challenge us to pray
for those who face despair,
and in love's name make us
your answer to our prayer.
Give us the grace to care and give
hope to the hopeless while they live.

© Copyright 2005 Stainer & Bell Ltd

Written 1 August 2005

Metre: 6.6.6.6.8 8.

Suggested Tune: LOVE UNKNOWN

Author's Note: Under the title *Shoah* the poet Harry Smart published a series of poems ostensibly about Noah and the ark but implicity concerned with the holocaust (Faber and Faber, 1993). I was especially moved by one text, *The man reads a testament*, in which Noah ceaselessly examines a document declaring how in spite of all pleas for intercession and deliverance even to the last hours, their father had perished in the waves. Noah laments. It is too late to pray.

44 The bush burns unconsumed

The bush burns unconsumed,
where God invites us all
to turn aside from fear and doubt
and hear and heed Love's call:

The call to make Love known
where hope has been betrayed
by prejudice and bitterness,
and people are afraid.

Where people are enslaved
by hatred and despair,
you send us, God of love, to be
your healing presence there.

And yet, how can we dare
to think the call is true:
that we should go into the world,
to speak and act for you?

Because the call is yours,
it is your word we hear:
your promise to be there with us
with love that conquers fear.

So send us where you will
and, never left alone,
we'll serve your justice, love and peace
and make your mercy known.

© Copyright 2005 Stainer & Bell Ltd

Written 22 August 2005

Metre: SM

Suggested Tune: FRANCONIA

Author's Note: A simple response to the story of Moses at the burning bush.

45   Jesus, whose wounding wins the world

Jesus, whose wounding wins the world,
yet leaves the world to go its way;
still only selfless love like yours
can hope to win the world today.

We want to leave your cross behind
and bathe in resurrection light,
beyond the reach of pain and fear,
and never know your grief's dark night.

We want to win the world to faith,
and bask in apostolic pride;
to prove our own ways true and claim
almighty God is on our side.

But you and your apostles dared
to face earth's stark reality,
to bear the pain and taste defeat,
as evil claimed the victory.

Open our eyes to see the light
that still comes shining from your cross,
and so to understand love's power,
that dares to risk death's total loss.

Give us the faith to live or die,
to serve in hope but dare to fail;
and through our humble faithfulness,
let love, your love alone, prevail.

© Copyright 2005 Stainer & Bell Ltd

Written 9 December 2005

Metre: LM

Suggested Tune: TRURO

Author's Note: A poem of Paul Celan has the lines, as translated by John Felstiner:

> wound wondrous gain
> of a world
>
> (from poem beginning 'Wan-voiced, / flayed from the depths', from *Selected Poems and Prose of Paul Celan*, translated by John Felstiner. Norton, 2001)

which sums up for me the triumph of the Cross. In an anti-war poem by Marianne Moore, *Keeping Their World Large*, she quotes the Reverend James Gordon Gilkey:

> 'If Christ and the apostles died in vain,
> I'll die in vain with them.'
>
> (from a letter printed in *The New York Times*, 7 June 1944)

So, this text arises out of the temptation to Christian triumphalism.

46 The baby sleeps in mother-love's strong arms

The baby sleeps in mother-love's strong arms,
she holds him anxiously against her heart,
as innocents are killed and parents grieve.

Earthquake and storm, war and indifference,
tear love apart with ruthless disregard,
and hopeless grief can see no reason why.

This child lies here, secure, as mother-love
infuses strength to share earth's grief and bear,
in innocence, the anger that will kill.

Friendless, alone, hanging in helplessness,
he too will shout against the grief and pain
of all the world, appealing, 'My God, why?'

Let us receive this child, and realise
the child in us, and find the innocence
that dares to take love at its word and trust.

God's mother-love continues through all joy
and deepest grief; it keeps in its own heart
– and will not lose – each single infant born.

© Copyright 2005 Stainer & Bell Ltd

Written 7 November 2005

Metre: 10.10.10.

Author's Note: This text is adapted from a poem originally created for a Christmas card, 2005. Appropriate for commemoration of the Holy Innocents.

Paul Hughes (1983–)

1. The ba-by sleeps in mo-ther-love's strong arms, she holds him an-xious-ly a-gainst her heart, as in-no-cents are killed and par-ents grieve.

2. Earth-quake and storm, war and in-dif-fer-ence, tear love a-part with ruth-less dis-re-gard, and hope-less grief can see no rea-son why.

3. This child lies here, se-cure, as mo-ther-love con-tin-ues through all joy and deep-est grief; it keeps in its own heart — and will not lose — each sin-gle in-fant born.

4. Friend-less, a-lone, hang-ing in help-less-ness, he too will shout a-gainst the grief and pain of all the world, ap-peal-ing, 'My God, why?'

5. Let us re-ceive this child, and re-a-lise the child in us, and find the in-no-cence that dares to take love at its word and trust.

6. God's mo-ther-love in-fu-ses strength to share earth's grief and bear, in in-no-cence, the an-ger that will kill.

© Copyright 2011 Stainer & Bell Ltd

47 Great Holy Spirit, gentle injured dove

Great Holy Spirit, gentle injured dove,
    why do we flout
    and grieve your love?
It is as if we pluck your feathers out
    to leave you dead, and yet still dare
    to come to God with hollow prayer.

We share earth's prejudice and bitterness,
    its ruthless greed
    and selfishness,
that ride roughshod, ignoring human need,
    as tyranny and war release
    the forces that demolish peace.

Great Holy Spirit, purifying flame,
    devour all wrong;
    in power reclaim
our lives and seal the peace for which we long;
    inspire and use us, purified,
    to serve the love for which Christ died.

And if we fall again and fail to do
    all we intend,
    we plead with you:
come, like a rushing, powerful wind to bend
    our spirits to your will, and break
    false pride in us, for your love's sake.

Great Holy Spirit, claim our lives today,
    to do your will
    and clear the way
for worldwide justice and true peace, until
    you find your joy in us, and we
    delight in love's last victory!

© Copyright 2005 Stainer & Bell Ltd

Written 12 November 2005

Metre: 10.4.4.10.8 8.

Author's Note: George Herbert wrote (in this metre) a poem with the title *Ephes. 4.30 / Grieve not the Holy Spirit, &c.*, beginning 'And art thou grieved, sweet and sacred Dove ...'. This text, on the same theme, and in the same form, bears little relation to Herbert's poem, but was inspired by it.

Paul Hughes (1983–)

Great Holy Spirit, gentle injured dove, why do we flout and grieve your love? It is as if we pluck your feathers out to leave you dead, and yet still dare to come to God with hollow prayer.

-ry!

© Copyright 2011 Stainer & Bell Ltd

48 How blessed are those, our loving God

In memory of Trevor Hinxman

How blessed are those, our loving God,
who in your love have scaled the height
and, breaking through death's chilling cloud,
now stand in your eternal light.

Watch over us and all who still
walk in the valley and still face
the risks of life, with death to come:
hold us in your sustaining grace.

We trust to you, ourselves and those
whom we have loved and do love still;
those who have died, whom you have held
in deeper love, and always will.

Our mortal flesh is weak and frail,
we falter but, as years increase,
Lord guide us to the peak at last,
to view the landscape of your peace.

Then we shall stand with them and praise
your love for ever strong and true;
as you have made us for yourself,
we trust, with them, to rest in you.

© Copyright 2005 Stainer & Bell Ltd

Written 22 December 2005

Metre: LM

Suggested Tune: WINCHESTER NEW

Author's Note: In 1991 I wrote a hymn text based on thoughts from Augustine's *Confessions*: 'How blessed are all the saints, our God, / who having crossed the troubled sea'. I then adapted Augustine's ideas as a prayer following the committal at the graveside or crematorium. Then, ministering in Windermere, and particularly when the person who had died had been a keen hill walker or climber, it seemed appropriate to adopt a climbing metaphor. I used the adapted prayer for a few years and, in December 2005, at the service for Trevor Hinxman, who had walked his dog up many a hill, even when his health had made it more and more difficult. It was soon after that service that I thought to turn the adapted prayer into a hymn.

49 Loving God, like a father or mother

Loving God, like a father or mother,
you have loved us all perfectly,
and you teach us your love for each other
as the children of your family.
Love that made us, Love that saved us,
Love that still inspires our prayer and praise:
Trinity of love, in our love,
show your love to all the world.

Loving Jesus, you came as our brother
and for love's sake you lived and died;
you command us to love one another,
and to love our neighbours far and wide.
Chorus

Holy Spirit, by your inspiration
keep love's joy in our hearts ablaze;
let us share in your love's jubilation
till the whole earth shares our endless praise.
Chorus

© Copyright 2006 Stainer & Bell Ltd

Written 5 June 2006

Metre: 10.8.10.9. and Chorus 8.9.8.7.

Suggested Tune: SING HOSANNA

Author's Note: A simple attempt to give expression to God's love in Trinity, and to connect it with the way we live in the world. We cannot truly respond to this threefold love unless we live in the power of it and share it, ultimately, with the whole world.

50 Jesus, God's precious child on earth

Jesus, God's precious child on earth,
you lived and loved and died.
In you, to prove what we were worth,
God's love was crucified.
You did not relish sacrifice
or take death in your stride,
but in deep sorrow paid love's price:
accused, betrayed, denied.

You broke the bread in your distress,
which would for ever be
the sign of your own brokenness
nailed up on Calvary.
You said in anguish, pouring wine,
'Remember what I do;
let this for ever be the sign
of my blood shed for you.'

And still, today, we break the bread
and drink the wine again,
remembering still the love that bled:
as true here, now as then.
Remembering gives us strength to bear
grief, pain or loneliness;
your presence gives us love to share
with neighbours in distress.

So now we praise your love which chose
to face death's total loss,
and called forgiveness down on those
who nailed you to the cross.
Here now your love, so sure and true,
which broke through death's dark night,
dares us to live or die for you:
our dread and our delight!

© Copyright 2006 Stainer & Bell Ltd

Written 24 June 2006

Metre: CMD

Suggested Tunes: THIRD MODE MELODY and KINGSFOLD

Author's Note: Preaching, I suggested that when Jesus broke the bread at his last meal with his disciples, he was in great anguish. He was saying, in effect, 'Look! Look! This bread is my body! My body is going to be broken like this!' When he passed round the wine, he was saying, 'Look! Look! This is my blood.' It was a huge and anguished metaphor, as he faced the coming horror. This text was sung approaching communion.

51 Give us, great Christ, out of your majesty

Give us, great Christ, out of your majesty,
the hearts of lions, ever brave and strong,
which dare to take their stand and constantly
speak up for truth and love our whole life long.

But let us not succumb to cheap false pride
or claim our strength and courage as our own;
with you we stand and take life in our stride,
but miss life's purpose if we strive alone.

Give us, dear Christ, love's wise naïvety,
the innocence of lambs, their harmlessness,
which does no hurt, but in humility
displays God's power in childlike helplessness.

But let us not succumb to faithless fear,
as though we face the harsh world all alone;
your love sustains us, you are ever near
and give us strength to make your mercy known.

Afraid or fearless give us faith to dare,
as lambs or lions, still to follow you;
in strength or weakness, help us all to share
your love and truth in all we say or do.

© Copyright 2006 Stainer & Bell Ltd

Written 19 September 2006

Metre: 10.10.10.10.

Suggested Tune: MAGDA

Author's Note: I was preaching at the United Reformed Church in Heswall, Wirral, after a week's exhibition and study for schools of C. S. Lewis's *The Lion, the Witch and the Wardrobe*. I took up the theme of Aslan, the lion, taking the place of Edmund, who had been condemned to death.

52   Christ, hold us in your loving arms

Christ, hold us in your loving arms,
like infants, sinless and wide-eyed;
fill us with childlike innocence
and undermine our grown-up pride.

Give us faith's naïve confidence
which sees earth's dark reality,
but dares love's simple way of truth
to challenge hate and enmity.

Give us your childlike trust in God,
which gave you strength to face the cross,
where truthful love and innocence
came up against death's total loss.

You chose that way for sheer delight
in simple truth, as sure and great
as God's unfathomable love,
far deeper than earth's deepest hate.

Show us God's heart, where grief meets joy,
and when our faith seems all in vain
restore again our simple trust
in God who shares all human pain.

Against the evils of the world,
help us to trust your truth and be
persistent signs of healing love,
through faith's profound simplicity.

© Copyright 2006 Stainer & Bell Ltd

Written 30 September 2006

Metre: LM

Suggested Tunes: EISENACH and FULDA

Author's Note: Following the reading of *Job* 2:1–10, *Hebrews* 1:1–4, 5–12 and *Mark* 10:13–16, the preaching was about suffering and innocence.

53 Make us your prophets, Lord

Make us your prophets, Lord,
who truly hear your word,
which fires us with your Spirit's inspiration.
In all we say and do
prove that your love is true,
the hope and source of peace for every nation.

And when we fail to love
or set ourselves above
our neighbours with their different ways of seeing,
bring us with all our pride
where Jesus, crucified,
for love of all committed his whole being.

Give us his love that shares
our neighbours' pain, and dares
to suffer enmity and condemnation.
Whether we live or die
help us to prophesy,
proclaiming peace and reconciliation.

Though we live quietly,
with no authority,
yet feeble faith in us may show your goodness;
and though we may not see
how crucial it may be,
our faltering love may show your loving kindness.

In faith and hope we pray,
use us to serve that day
when bigotry and hatred are defeated,
when perfect peace is won
and lasting justice done,
with love's eternal promises completed.

© Copyright 2006 Stainer & Bell Ltd

Written 23 October 2006

Metre: 6 6.11.D.

Suggested Tune: DOWN AMPNEY

Author's Note: The hymn came out of reading *Numbers* 11:24–29. It is about Christian prophetic ministry, but at the time of writing I was disturbed by government ministers, as well as the press, making much of Muslim women wearing the veil, calling it a 'sign of separation'. It seemed like playing into the hands of bigots and extremists, and made me think of Germany in the early 1930s. Chosen for the new Methodist hymnbook, *Singing the Faith*, published in 2011.

54   The voice that makes the world go dark

The voice that makes the world go dark
for families that wait in dread,
is heard so many thousand times,
and says, 'The one you love is dead.'

As we remember those who died
in wars long gone, and grieve their loss,
the nations go to war again,
still nailing mercy to the cross.

As we seek justice for ourselves,
justice for others is denied;
God's sons and daughters lose their lives
and innocence is crucified.

Now, God, as nations strive for power,
forgive the unreality
that trusts in war to bring us peace,
against the facts of history.

As we remember, with regret,
the brave and helpless who have died,
forgive the hardness of our hearts,
our careless prejudice and pride.

God, give the rulers of the world
the naïve wisdom to decease
from wasting human lives in war,
and take the risk of making peace.

© Copyright 2007 Stainer & Bell Ltd

Written 12 January 2007

Metre: LM

Suggested Tune: O WALY WALY

Author's Note: I was struck very forcibly by the then Prime Minister's suggestion that peacemaking was the 'easy option'. I was reminded that even Winston Churchill said that 'Jaw, jaw was better than war, war.' Peacemaking is by no means the easy option. An uncle of mine was killed in the First World War. His brother, another uncle, much later wrote about the day when the family received the news. Their father had been called home from the coalface, asking the foreman, 'Is it the lad?' At the end of the shift, the younger brother left the coalface for home and, seeing the curtains drawn, it was as though a voice in his head was repeatedly saying, 'Your brother is dead.' That story coloured my view of Remembrance Sunday.

55 Man on a donkey, come to town

For Jane Weedon
Palm Sunday, 1 April

Man on a donkey, come to town,
although you wear no monarch's crown
the people round you shout and sing,
and greet you as their saviour king.

Is this how saviours stake their claim?
Is this how kings secure their fame?
Do donkeys give them dignity
or demonstrate their majesty?

Who but a fool dares such a thing,
to be a donkey-riding king?
Small wonder that you faced defeat
and died with nails in hands and feet.

And yet we praise your foolishness
and, worshipping your helplessness,
we see in powerless love that dies
God's power, unfathomably wise.

So, Servant Lord, make us today
love's fools, with wisdom to convey
God's power in helplessness, and be
your truly wise community.

© Copyright 2007 Stainer & Bell Ltd

Written 12 March 2007

Metre: LM

Suggested Tune: BRESLAU

Author's Note: Jane Weedon was inducted to the pastorate of the Free Church with Panshanger and Woodhall Lane United Reformed Churches, Welwyn Garden City, on Palm Sunday, 1 April 2007. It seemed not inappropriate to read, not only about Palm Sunday, but also from the first chapter of *1 Corinthians*, where Paul writes about the foolishness of the cross, God's foolishness being wiser than human wisdom, and about being fools for Christ's sake.

56 Be with us, Servant Lord

For Susan Durber

Be with us, Servant Lord,
whose full self-sacrifice
has taught us what it means to love
and dare to pay love's price.

Here, as we teach and learn,
increase humility;
for only those who humble self
unveil love's mystery.

You made love's mystery known
through storyteller's art;
the wisely simple understood
and took love's truth to heart.

As we explore love's truth
and share our stories here,
give us your unpretentious art
to make your Gospel clear.

Make us so simply wise
that we may comprehend
the vast unfathomed love of God
you trusted to the end.

Be with us, Servant Lord,
and make us servants too,
who, teaching, never cease to learn
God's deathless love in you.

© Copyright 2007 Stainer & Bell Ltd

Written 13 March 2007

Metre: SM

Suggested Tune: DUNDRENNAN

Author's Note: Susan Durber was to be inducted as Principal of Westminster College, Cambridge in September 2007. This text was written for Caryl Micklem's tune, DUNDRENNAN, which she chose. The themes of teaching, learning and storytelling were also her choice.

57 God, you see your pleas for justice

God, you see your pleas for justice
swamped by inhumanity,
overwhelmed by cheap indifference,
still allowing slavery.
With such evil years behind us,
how can we escape the blame,
when your children, in your image,
still bear cruelty and shame?

Husbands, wives and little children,
separated, in despair,
serve as slaves, to meet the comforts
of the rich who never care.
Innocent and orphaned children,
are abused and brutalised,
forced to fight in ruthless conflict,
robbed of childhood, terrorised.

Girls and women are exploited,
bought and sold, despised and shamed;
others, hungry and in danger,
are defrauded and then blamed:
friendless in a foreign country,
homeless, hounded and misused,
where they hoped to find a welcome
hope and safety are refused.

God, forgive us, teach us mercy,
make us feel the hopelessness
of the brutally exploited,
in their grief and helplessness.
Judge us, God, till every nation
puts an end to slavery,
till you see, in peace and justice,
every living soul set free.

© Copyright 2007 Stainer & Bell Ltd

Written 20 March 2007

Metre: 8.7.8.7.D.

Suggested Tune: EBENEZER (TON-Y-BOTEL)

Author's Note: It being the 200th anniversary of the abolition of the slave trade in the British Empire, one felt compelled to approach the difficult theme of slavery: remembering that the abolition of the trade did not then abolish slavery, and particularly realising that slavery is still a reality, even in our own country. So, one could not write a happy hymn on the theme.

58 Mary, friend of Jesus, Mary Magdalen

Mary, friend of Jesus, Mary Magdalen,
tell us all what Jesus came and did for you.
He came and healed me of my deep despair,
took away my darkness and the light broke through!

Mary, friend of Jesus, Mary Magdalen,
tell us what you saw that day on Calvary.
I saw his anguish, hanging on the cross,
and stood there so helpless, full of misery.

Mary, friend of Jesus, Mary Magdalen,
tell us what you felt when you came to his tomb.
Deep grief and sorrow, then grief deeper still,
when the grave was empty and his body gone!

Mary, friend of Jesus, Mary Magdalen,
tell us all what happened, tell us all again!
Blinded by tears, I did not recognise
Jesus speaking to me, till he said my name!

Then I saw and knew him and was filled with joy;
he had called me 'Mary' and, with that one word,
I was restored to faith and hope again,
and I ran back shouting, 'I have seen the Lord!'

Mary, first apostle of the risen Christ,
Jesus calls our names, and we will be like you;
we will proclaim his love for all the world,
we will spread your joy, as his apostles too.

© Copyright 2007 Stainer & Bell Ltd

Written 1 May 2007

Metre: 11.11.11.11.

Suggested Tune: NOËL NOUVELET

Author's Note: Originally written for a service I led at the United Reformed Church at Heswall on 'the friends of Jesus' and later much revised. Men and boys sing the words in roman type; women and girls, those in italics; all sing the final verse, in bold type.

59 Loving God, your radiant sunlight

For the hundredth anniversary of Thornton Hough United Reformed Church

Loving God, your radiant sunlight*
fills our hearts with joy and praise;
from eternity its brightness
guides us through our passing days.
In its glory you have shown us
love in all its majesty,
love which lived and died in Jesus,
sharing frail humanity.

In love's resurrected splendour
you have called us to exceed
charity with costly justice,
filling every human need.
Some have tried to meet your challenge,
through their faith and industry,
giving others just employment,
self-esteem, security.

Though full justice still eludes us,
keep our faltering hope alive,
trusting, through success or failure,
faith and love will still survive.
Here, where we for years have worshipped,
as we hear again today
love's demand for truth and justice,
give us courage to obey.

Loving God, as we still worship,
meeting with you in this place,
as we praise your endless mercies,
make us windows of your grace.
Let your glory, shining through us,
colour all we say and do,
till, when truth and justice triumph,
all creation praises you.

© Copyright 2007 Stainer & Bell Ltd

Written 15 May 2007

Metre: 8.7.8.7.D.

Suggested Tune: ABBOT'S LEIGH

Author's Note: The United Reformed Church (originally Congregational) at Thornton Hough was built by the first Lord Leverhulme, the village being down the road from his home, Thornton Hall. 2007 marked the hundredth anniversary of the building and, on the occasion of the celebration, a new window was unveiled in memory of the third and last Lord Leverhulme. I was invited to produce a hymn for the occasion. When I asked what I should write, someone suggested that there ought to be a mention of soap.

*Early in its history Lord Leverhulme's factory in Port Sunlight produced Sunlight soap.

60   Perfect sunlit dawning

Perfect sunlit dawning
of a perfect day;
joy pervades this morning,
driving grief away.
All was grim and hopeless
through the grievous night;
now despair and darkness
vanish in the light.

Love had been defeated:
scorned and crucified,
faith and hope were cheated,
truth was falsified;
death eclipsed the brightness
of the light God gave;
crucified and helpless,
God was in the grave.

Now in glory, springing
out of emptiness,
Christ comes risen, bringing
joy from bitterness;
Love returns, triumphant,
truth comes back to stay;
faith and hope, exultant,
greet the dazzling day.

© Copyright 2007 Stainer & Bell Ltd

Written 3 August 2007

Metre: 6.5.6.5.D.

Suggested Tune: RUTH (Smith)

Author's Note: On 3 August, I suddenly felt the urge to write these Easter words. The tune which came to mind was a favourite from childhood, RUTH, which we would sing on summer evenings, with the sun shining through the stained-glass windows, in Alexandra Road Congregational Church, Blackpool, where my father was minister.

61 Yes, Mary, we have greeted

Yes, Mary, we have greeted
the arrival of your child,
who came with God's compassion
to a world so harsh and wild.
He grew to serve love's purpose
in ways you could not share,
but when his flesh was broken
you knew such deep despair.

And yet we hail you, Mary,
as a mother truly blest,
whose child still shines upon us,
making God's love manifest:
your son who bore earth's sorrow
and died to heal earth's pain,
yet, as a humble servant,
still comes in love, to reign.

As we recall his coming
into troubled Bethlehem,
we pray for true goodwill there
and peace in Jerusalem.
We long to see the healing
of earth's hostility,
the end of fear and hatred
through his nativity.

If only we would let him
break our prejudice and pride,
and fill us with compassion
like his own, which loved and died;
if we dared recognise him
in every infant's birth,
there could be peace with justice
for every child on earth.

© Copyright 2008 Stainer & Bell Ltd

Written 10 January 2008

Metre: 7.7.7.7.7.6.7.6.

Suggested Tune: CHARTRES

Author's Note: This was written for a Christmas card: rather early for Christmas 2008.

62   Eternal God, you live and move

Eternal God, you live and move
in light too bright for human sight,
and yet the wonder of your love
illuminated earth's dark night,
when you in Jesus dared to trust
transcendent glory to our dust.

He came from love's deep mystery
to be a child on earth and learn
the truth of our humanity;
to share its joy and bear its pain,
and then, in anguish on the cross,
to face the dread of total loss.

Your love, embodied, left to die,
found grief and pain too hard to bear;
in deep distress he asked you 'why?'
– why you, his God, forsook him there.
Love cried to Love with one last breath
and gave himself to you in death.

And from that darkest place on earth,
your light has poured across the years;
faith, hope and love are brought to birth,
and joy springs up through grief and tears.
Love stoops to conquer earth's despair;
we reach the cross and find you there.

© Copyright 2008 Stainer & Bell Ltd

Written 17 March 2008

Metre: 8.8.8.8.8 8.

Suggested Tune: MELITA

Author's Note: I wanted some words to express my understanding of the Incarnation.

63 Columba, long ago in Ireland

Columba, long ago in Ireland,
your battle for your selfish ends
left many dead and many orphaned.
How could you ever make amends?
You brought your faith across the sea
and in repentance vowed to claim
as many souls as died, to be
baptised and bear Christ's holy name.

You travelled and proclaimed the Gospel
in Scotland and the islands round;
you preached the word to chiefs and people,
and made each place God's holy ground;
your inspiration gave new heart
to politics, where faith was tried;
you wrote and taught, you played your part
for justice, as you prophesied.

Columba, in the name of Jesus,
to serve our God, we follow you,
and where the Holy Spirit leads us
we trust that we shall prove as true.
Remembering you, we dare believe
that serving Love's great Trinity,
though feeble saints, we will receive
our share of faith's integrity.

Great God, Columba's inspiration,
whose grace gave him the power to be
your prophet, challenging a nation
and overcoming enmity;
make us as faithful in our day,
through us let holy love increase,
may we like him live as we pray,
and work for justice, love and peace.

© Copyright 2008 Stainer & Bell Ltd

Written 12 May 2008

Metre: 9.8.9.8.8.8.8.8.

Suggested Tune: YE BANKS AND BRAES

Author's Note: The Church of Scotland congregation which worships in a basement room of Liverpool Anglican Cathedral was celebrating a Fàilte, and asked me to compose some words about Columba, to a Scottish tune.

64   Great God of love, you know us through and through

For David Powell

Great God of love, you know us through and through,
and see the flaws in all we claim as true;
transcending certainties our dogmas raise,
you shame the prejudice that mars our praise.

Christ, whom our bigotry still crucifies
and on whose cross our biased judgement dies,
raise us from rivalries that pride defends,
unite us, as your witnesses and friends.

Empowering Spirit, show us how to be
sisters and brothers, God's true family;
spread your great wings around us, gentle dove,
heal our divisions with relentless love.

Eternal Trinity, fulfil our prayer:
give us responsive love like yours to share:
united, perfect, ever bound yet free,
where peace and joy exclude all enmity.

And then your vibrant Church will find the grace
to love each friend and stranger, and embrace
the hope of peace and justice, far and wide,
with love triumphant, flawless, glorified!

© Copyright 2008 Stainer & Bell Ltd

Written 19 July 2008

Metre: 10 10.10 10.

Suggested Tune: BLACKBIRD LEYS

Author's Note: David Powell requested a hymn for the Week of Prayer for Christian Unity. In responding I tried to express something of what I believe about the things that divide us, and the persistent love of God in Trinity, which is the source of our unity. More than that, I believe the love of God demands our unity, in which we will be 'bound yet free'.

65 Spirit, coming in the splendour

Spirit, coming in the splendour
when the sun is at its height;
you come too, as earth's befriender
with the moon and stars at night;
with the wind that stirs the ocean,
breath that calms the troubled sea:
source of joy and deep emotion,
Love's profoundest mystery.

Through the forests, over beaches,
scaling mountains, crossing plains,
your creative passion reaches,
your tremendous love sustains.
Every creature is encircled
by your love, in earth and sky,
by your tenderness enfolded
while they live and when they die.

From the wrongs that should appal us,
from destructiveness and greed,
loving Holy Spirit, call us
to the love we sorely need;
then in love for your creation
and our care for all the earth,
we shall find our own salvation
and discover our true worth.

Spirit, through all things around us,
let us keep your love in sight,
and in all that lives surround us
with your infinite delight;
then, like Jesus, through his passion,
risking censure, grief or blame,
help us, too, serve God's creation
and sustain love's tender flame.

© Copyright 2008 Stainer & Bell Ltd

Written 12 August 2008

Metre: 8.7.8.7.D.

Suggested Tune: ODE TO JOY

Author's Note: This text arose out of a second reading of Martin Palmer's *Living Christianity* (Element Books, 1993) and begins from his quotation of a poem from *The Black Book of Carmarthen*: 'I am the wind that breathes upon the sea, I am the wave of the ocean ...' (p.82). Martin Palmer also refers a number of times to the Nestorian Christian idea of Christ becoming flesh, suffering and dying, so making 'the whole world know that a human life is as precarious as the candle flame' (p.177). This text is an attempt to express the desire all human beings ought to have, to serve the needs of creation rather than to use creation simply for our own ends.

66 In music we express delight

In music we express delight,
our joy and love of life take wing;
like birds, we soar towards the height
of love's perfection when we sing;
with voice and instrument we raise
exultant rhapsodies of praise!

In music, too, we sound the grief
of human agony and loss,
which Jesus shared without relief
when he was dying on the cross;
our music echoes his last prayer,
drawn out of earth's profound despair.

But then our music's depth and height
combine in one the two extremes,
as grief meets joy and both unite,
composing new and stronger themes,
in which the dirge of death's dark night
transposes into sheer delight!

So instruments and voices raise,
in unison and harmony,
new variations in glad praise
of Love's eternal Trinity;
and as our mortal praise ascends
Love's vaster music never ends.

© Copyright 2008 Stainer & Bell Ltd

Written 6 August 2008

Metre: 8.8.8.8.8 8.

Suggested Tune: AFORO-KWABI

Author's Note: I was given the honour of being invited to become Honorary President of the United Reformed Church Musicians Guild, and it was suggested that I might be inspired to write an appropriate hymn.

AFORO-KWABI

Paul Benson (1951–)

In music we express delight, our joy and love of life take wing; like birds, we soar towards the height of love's perfection when we sing; with voice and instrument we raise exultant rhapsodies of praise!

© Copyright 2011 Stainer & Bell Ltd

67 Look! I'm so light

SO LIGHT
Alan Gaunt (1935–)

Look! I'm so light, I'm floating away; don't let's be serious, I just want to play. Don't tell me your sorrows, I can't share your pain; don't tell me your troubles, I can't take the strain. I only like laughter, I've no time for tears; to all cries of anguish I just close my ears. Love make us wise, yes, this is our prayer: for all of our neighbours, yes, Love make us care, yes, Love make us care.

© Copyright 2011 Stainer & Bell Ltd

Look! I'm so light,
I'm floating away;
don't let's be serious,
I just want to play.

Don't tell me your sorrows, I can't share your pain;
don't tell me your troubles, I can't take the strain.
I only like laughter, I've no time for tears;
to all cries of anguish I just close my ears.

Look! I'm so light,
I'm floating away;
don't let's be serious,
I just want to play.

Don't talk about Jesus who died on the cross;
don't talk about hunger, or sorrow and loss.
If people are dying, in pain and despair,
don't tell me about it, don't ask me to care.

Look! I'm so light,
I'm floating away;
don't let's be serious,
I just want to play.

And yet if I love you, could I be so blind?
If you were in trouble would I be unkind?
No, surely compassion would pierce like a dart,
and bring me to earth with a weight on my heart.

Love make me wise,
and let me be found
head out of the clouds
with feet on the ground.

So let us together come right down to earth,
and following Jesus for all we are worth,
let's love one another and let us all share
our love with our neighbours. Let this be our prayer:

Love make us wise,
yes, this is our prayer:
for all of our neighbours,
yes, Love make us care.

© Copyright 2008 Stainer & Bell Ltd

Written 7 August 2008

Metre: 11 11.11 11. and Chorus 4.5.6.5.

Suggested Tune: SO LIGHT

Author's Note: This text arose from a short adaptation of George MacDonald's *The Light Princess*, in which a baby princess is deprived of all her gravity, physical and emotional, by the spell of a wicked aunt. All her life, she floats through the air and can take nothing seriously, until she is saved by the love of a prince who is prepared to give up his life for her.

68 Let's count the stars

Let's count the stars, perhaps when we have finished,
we'll see how near we are to knowing God;
God who is far beyond all we can fathom,
and yet as close as every breath we breathe.
Let's count the stars and if we ever finish
we might just understand the love of God.

Let's count the stars, and after all our lifetime,
when we have done, there will be millions more.
Just so, God's love is vaster than creation,
deeper and surer than the universe.
Let's count the stars and if we ever finish
we might just understand the love of God.

The love of God exceeds imagination,
and yet enfolds us gently from our birth,
sharing our greatest joy and deepest sorrow,
holding us always in huge tenderness.
Let's not count stars, for we can never finish,
but simply trust the endless love of God.

© Copyright 2009 Stainer & Bell Ltd

Written 30 January 2009

Metre: 11.10.11.10. and Chorus 11.10.

Suggested Tune: SOM STRANDEN

Author's Note: This was written for all-age worship, arising out of *Isaiah* 40:25–26: 'To whom then will you compare me, or who is my equal? says the Holy One. Lift up your eyes on high and see: Who created these [the stars]?' (*NRSV*).

69 The true Church is found where God's purpose is sovereign

A HYMN FOR JOHN CALVIN AFTER 500 YEARS
Written for Susan Durber

The true Church is found where God's purpose is sovereign,
where people acknowledge God's will as supreme;
each under God's governance, trusting God's greatness,
beyond all the splendour earth's conquerors could dream!

The true Church is found where its preachers sincerely,
with true hearts and minds, are proclaiming God's Word;
where people are hearing and truly responding,
and yearning to live in the truth they have heard.

The true Church is found where the bread is still broken,
received by the people at Christ's own command,
with Christ truly present for those who receive it,
as though it is served by his own wounded hand.

The true Church is found where God's people acknowledge
the crucified Christ and submit to his call;
his chosen ones serve him, whose service is freedom,
and though worlds should perish, his Church shall not fall.

The true Church is found where God's people, united,
are joined in obedience to Christ, in whose name,
with love and goodwill they put trust in each other,
and prove by their own love, the love they proclaim!

The true Church is found where, without condemnation,
Christ's people love others, and hatred is healed.
They look for the good and seek Christ in each neighbour,
till Love's hidden purpose for all is revealed.

© Copyright 2009 Stainer & Bell Ltd

Written 7 February 2009

Metre: 12.11.12.11.

Suggested Tune: ST CATHERINE'S COURT

Author's Note: A hymn text to celebrate 500 years since the birth of John Calvin. Each verse takes up a theme that can be found in John Calvin's teaching. However, Karl Barth said, 'being taught by Calvin means entering into dialogue with him ... Calvin wants to teach and not just say something that we will repeat. The aim ... is a dialogue that may end with the taught saying something very different from what Calvin said but that they learned from or, better, through him.' (Karl Barth, translated by Geoffrey W. Bromiley: *The Theology of John Calvin*, p.4. Eerdmans, 1995.)

70   Saint David was dying

For St David's, Eastham

Saint David was dying,
and yet he was preaching,
forbidding his people to grieve:
'Stop weeping, my brothers,
don't mourn me, my sisters,
rejoice in the truth we believe;
keep faith and be humble,
let your deeds resemble
the little things witnessed in me.'
His words were so gentle,
sincere and so simple,
yet true and profound as could be.

So, God, keep us serving,
courageous, rejoicing
and faithful in service, we pray:
still trusting and sharing
your love and still daring
to be saints, like David, today.

God, fill us with wonder,
as we now remember
your saints who have served down the years.
In search of love's kingdom,
wherever truth led them,
they served you through laughter and tears.
So now, let us follow,
through joy or through sorrow;
uphold us through pleasure or pain.
Then, as your truth leads us
and your power sustains us,
we'll live to establish love's reign.

So, God, keep us serving,
courageous, rejoicing
and faithful in service, we pray:
still trusting and sharing
your love and still daring
to be saints, like David, today.

© Copyright 2009 Stainer & Bell Ltd

Written 20 February 2009

Metre: 6.6.8.6.6.8.D. and Chorus 6 6.8.D.

Suggested Tune: OLWEN

Author's Note: This was written for St David's United Reformed Church, Eastham, when St David's Day fell on a Sunday in 2009. The underlying theme is that all who belong to Christ are saints, however naughty or feeble. I believe that David was probably preaching from *Philippians* 4:4–9.

71   Great God of Moses, so tenderly yearning

For Hilary Bell

Great God of Moses, so tenderly yearning,
feeling earth's sorrow, its pain and despair,
we turn aside, where your love's fire, still burning,
calls us to prove your compassion and care.

God, who are we to accomplish your purpose?
Yet you engage us, to venture and dare,
trusting your promise, to us as to Moses:
'I will be there for you, always be there.'

Christ, you encounter us when least expected,
as with the woman who came to the well;
she, by your people, despised and rejected,
found her self-worth and had good news to tell.

Christ, who by dying attained love's perfection,
bearing the anguish of all those who grieve;
this is your promise, through love's resurrection:
life-giving water for all who believe.

Spirit of God, ever sure yet surprising,
spring up in us and refresh all our days;
colour our lives with love's dying and rising,
hope's promised freedom, and faith's endless praise!

© Copyright 2009 Stainer & Bell Ltd

Written 4 April 2009

Metre: 11.10.11.10.

Suggested Tune: EPIPHANY HYMN

Author's Note: This text was written for Hilary Bell on the occasion of her ordination, 4 July 2009. Her chosen readings were *Exodus* 3:1–12 (the burning bush) and *John* 4:7–15 (the Samaritan woman at the well, and living water). Hilary said in her ordination statement that God appears when we least expect it and adds colour to our life. It was written for her chosen tune: EPIPHANY HYMN.

72 They ran and ran, so full of joy

They ran and ran, so full of joy,
as folk had never run,
so light of foot and unafraid:
their new life had begun!
They ran and ran to tell the world
what God's great love had done.

They ran and ran to tell the world
that Jesus, crucified,
had shown himself to them alive
and death had been defied!
They ran, so full of joy, to spread
their good news far and wide!

Their news has travelled down the years,
and stirs our hearts today;
the risen Jesus lives with us
and, as we trust and pray,
exultant resurrection love
can take our fear away.

So let us run out fearlessly,
alive and full of grace:
the friends of Jesus, full of hope
and ready to embrace
his cause of justice, joy and peace
for all the human race.

© Copyright 2009 Stainer & Bell Ltd

Written 17 April 2009

Metre: 8.6.8.6.8.6.

Suggested Tune: SHELTERED DALE

Author's Note: This text came out of *A Fragment* in Margaret Cropper's *Selected Poems*. The poem was read in worship on the third Sunday of Easter, and these words were written to follow it. *A Fragment* begins

> ... So they ran down, they ran down
> As never men folk ran.

It ends

> They ran down, even as a stream runs down,
> Lovely and wise, and without fear or sorrow.

(from Margaret Cropper: *Selected Poems*. Titus Wilson and Son Ltd, 1958)

73 We speak so many words

We speak so many words
to name you, hidden God.
We make our metaphors
and think we have a hold
on what you mean and who you are,
as if we held the farthest star!

In vast humility
you let yourself be named,
and in the words we say
some essence is contained
of love that cannot be confined
and truth beyond all reach of mind.

But once your love on earth
broke through our metaphors,
to share our life and death,
oppressed by our despair;
and, after anguish on the cross,
passed through the depths of total loss.

But from love's tomb there sounds,
down through the centuries,
a meaning that confounds
death's fathomless abyss.
Beyond all human metaphors,
faith trusts love's secret and adores!

© Copyright 2009 Stainer & Bell Ltd

Written 30 July 2009

Metre: 6.6.6.6.8 8.

Suggested Tune: LAWES PSALM 47

Author's Note: This came out of my reading of a Paul Celan poem:

> A rumbling: it is
> Truth itself
> walked among
> men,
> amidst the
> metaphor squall.

(from *14 Poems from Breathturn, Selected Poems and Prose of Paul Celan*, translated by John Felstiner. Norton, 2001)

Christians and theologians have always been tempted to make idols of their ideas and images of God, and have too often insisted that their own dogmas must be believed. But in truth, everything we say about God in human language falls far short of God's reality. And yet somewhere behind our storm of metaphors, the truth rumbles like distant thunder and, in Jesus Christ, we dare to believe, did walk among us. Yet still mysterious, beyond our comprehension.

74   Great God of love, you share your children's pain

Great God of love, you share your children's pain,
you grieve with those who mourn for thousands slain;
each one, uniquely precious in your sight,
is found and held in your eternal light.

Some fought and died, both brave and terrified,
remembered now with grief or proper pride;
and still, in our own time, so many more
risk death or lifelong injury in war.

Civilians lose their lives in war as well,
and innocents bear hunger, grief and hell,
as we go on, embroiled in cruel wars,
and dare to think the cause we fight is yours.

God, bring your children through the moral maze,
where in past years, and still in recent days,
the tribes and nations, suffering death and loss,
have failed to reach love's centre at the cross.

There, Jesus faced earth's hatred and false pride,
there, loving to the bitter end, he died;
there, in his dying love, he represents
the dead, the wounded and the innocents.

God, as we come with our remembrance prayers,
challenge your people to the faith that dares
bravely to work with Christ for love's increase,
and live or die for justice, truth and peace.

© Copyright 2009 Stainer & Bell Ltd

Written 1 October 2009

Metre: 10 10.10 10.

Suggested Tune: VALIANT HEARTS

Author's Note: Unable to sing 'O valiant hearts, who to your glory came ...', which seems to me to glorify war, I was asked to write words to the same tune. I trust that these words could be sung, not only by strict pacifists, but by all Christians who remember the war dead, but also yearn for justice and peace in the world.

75 We bring our thanks, our gracious God

We bring our thanks, our gracious God,
for past remembered years,
in which we shared our faith and hope
through times of joy and tears.
Together we have searched your word
and tried to prove it true
by living for our neighbours' good,
out of our love for you.

The prophets and the preachers came,
and with their eloquence,
they challenged us to take faith's risks,
with hope and confidence;
and always there were those who served
and worked hard constantly,
who helped us serve our neighbours' needs
and witness faithfully.

Sometimes we found our common cause,
and caught your Spirit's fire,
we shared the Gospel's hopefulness
and felt the Gospel's power.
At other times we spoke our minds
and frankly disagreed,
but through it all your grace remained,
your love was guaranteed.

Now, as the future beckons us
we put the past behind,
with some regret, but confident,
believing we will find
your grace as sure in years ahead,
your love, as always, true;
and for the future, as the past,
we put our trust in you.

© Copyright 2009 Stainer & Bell Ltd

Written 14 October 2009

Metre: CMD

Suggested Tune: KINGSFOLD

Author's Note: The South West Manchester Group of United Reformed and Baptist churches was breaking up, not because of difficulties, but for very positive reasons. Along with others, I was asked to write a hymn for the final service.

76   Help us, Jesus, to be like you

Help us, Jesus, to be like you:
loving, gentle, kind and true,
brave, but humble, in every way,
helpful in all that we do or say.

We are not as loving as we ought to be,
always treating other people graciously;
and not always gentle, and not kind and true,
not convincing others we belong to you.
Chorus

Often we are proud, and often sneer and frown,
we hurt other people, and we let you down;
spiteful and unhelpful in the things we do,
saying things we shouldn't say, we still hurt you.
Chorus

Though we often fail you, and we cause you pain,
you will never leave us and you will remain
our true friend for ever, and you will forgive
time and time again, as long as we shall live.
Chorus

Jesus, you have loved us well enough to die,
now we want to share your love, and this is why:
so that we can gladly live and speak for you,
always brave and humble, gentle, kind and true.

© Copyright 2009 Stainer & Bell Ltd

Written 27 October 2009

Metre: 11 11.11 11. and Chorus 8 7.8 9.

Suggested Tune: OVERCHURCH

Author's Note: I have to confess to being a little disturbed by the shallowness and unreality of some of the religious songs which children sing at school. This was an attempt at simplicity, with some sense of reality: and not simplistic.

OVERCHURCH

Tony Davies (1945–)

Help us, Jesus, to be like you: loving, gentle, kind and true, brave, but humble, in every way, helpful in all that we do or say. We are not as loving as we ought to be, always treating other people graciously; and not always gentle, and not kind and true, not convincing others we belong to you.

© Copyright 2011 Stainer & Bell Ltd

77 Mary gave birth to her child

Mary gave birth to her child
in a world so cruel and wild,
a brutal world full of pain,
in which young children are slain.
But the simple and the wise,
with sharp ears and seeing eyes,
came and found him where he lay,
Mary's child we greet today.

Yes, come to greet this infant,
and praise his newborn glory.
Before his helplessness
worship and adore,
and celebrate the power of innocence.

Mary kept her child secure
and, with Joseph, strong and sure,
all remained serene and calm,
they protected him from harm.
But when he was twelve years old,
she felt she was losing hold,
and she pondered in her heart,
as he seemed to draw apart.

Yet see how he amazes
the scholars in the temple.
Before his wisdom there
worship and adore,
and marvel at the power of innocence.

Later, Mary saw him die,
and she heard him ask God, 'Why?'
As she saw him hanging there,
did her breaking heart despair?
Had she birthed her child for this?
When she gave him his first kiss,
she most surely could not see
she would share such tragedy.

So, come and see him dying,
a victim of earth's evil.
Before his helplessness
worship and adore,
still marvel at the power of innocence.

Though a sword had pierced her heart,
she fulfilled a mother's part;
he, so lovely in her eyes,
grew up faithful, strong and wise.
So, through Mary's anxious fears,
through earth's grief and blinding tears;
through all sorrow, greet her boy,
born to give us endless joy.

Yes, come, you wise and simple,
to greet the Christmas infant.
Before his helplessness
worship and adore,
and celebrate the power of innocence.

© Copyright 2010 Stainer & Bell Ltd

Written 10 January 2010

Metre: 7 7.7 7.D. and Chorus 7.7.6.5.10.

Suggested Tune: SHEPHERDS' FIELD

Author's Note: Approaching the jollity and sentimentality of Christmas, it does not seem inappropriate to call to mind the ultimate consequences of the Incarnation. Hence, Mary's pain, the Cross, and a hint of Resurrection: through sorrow to ultimate joy.

SHEPHERDS' FIELD

Tony Davies (1945–)

Mary gave birth to her child in a world so cruel and wild, a brutal world full of pain, in which young children are slain. But the simple and the wise, with sharp ears and seeing eyes, came and found him where he lay, Mary's child we greet today. Yes, come to greet this infant, and praise his new-born glory. Before his helplessness worship and adore, and celebrate the power of innocence.

© Copyright 2011 Stainer & Bell Ltd

78 Don't let love fail, Lord

Paul Hughes (1983–)

1 When your children are in distress and grief becomes too much to bear;
when the world grows too dark and cold and people are left in despair;
when the havoc of war creates more anguish as thousands are slain;
when families, broken in heart, live on with unbearable pain:
Don't let love fail,

© Copyright 2011 Stainer & Bell Ltd

When your children are in distress
and grief becomes too much to bear;
when the world grows too dark and cold
and people are left in despair;
when the havoc of war creates
more anguish as thousands are slain;
when families, broken in heart,
live on with unbearable pain:
Don't let love fail, Lord,
we trust that your love will not fail.

In Gethsemane, dark and cold,
you, Jesus, were crushed by despair,
in darkness, let down by your friends,
you struggled in agonized prayer;
and pierced with cruel nails on the cross,
with all that you stood for denied,
there you felt forsaken by God,
yet trusted again, as you died.
Don't let love fail, Lord,
we trust that your love will not fail.

When people and nations run wild,
indulging the hatred they feel;
when we ourselves undermine love
with bitterness nothing can heal;
when neighbours are deep in distress
and we neither notice nor care;
Lord, bring us again to your cross,
and let your love challenge us there.
Don't let love fail, Lord,
we trust that your love will not fail.

There's no human anguish or pain
which you, in your love, do not share;
and all human grief and distress
you carry to God's heart in prayer;
there's no sorrow we can pass through,
no darkness or ultimate night,
which will not be brought to its end
in your resurrection delight.
Don't let love fail, Lord,
we trust that your love will not fail.

© Copyright 2010 Stainer & Bell Ltd

Written 25 January 2010

Metre: LMD and Chorus 5.8.

Author's Note: Reading about people's deep pain and sorrow, and the anguish of people affected by war and natural disaster, I uttered, in my helplessness, the desperate prayer: 'Don't let love fail, Lord.'

79 The silent night comes down

The silent night comes down
and all seems safe and calm;
his loving mother keeps
her newborn son from harm.
She holds him very close,
drawn by his quietness,
and lays him down to rest,
awed by his helplessness.

He sleeps now, quietly,
but when he wakes and cries
the power of innocence
will take her by surprise.
But what if storms should rage
and dogs of war run wild,
what measures could she take
to save her precious child?

Fear and frustrated power
build grim dividing walls;
suspicion, hatred, pride
stifle love's anguished calls.
And yet, divided, those
who dare to stretch out hands
in childlike innocence
will still hear love's demands.

This child who sleeps and cries,
grown simply wise, will dare
stand up to hate with love
and, facing deep despair,
will challenge earth to see,
through pain and grief's distress,
love's towering innocence,
love's power in helplessness.

© Copyright 2010 Stainer & Bell Ltd

Written 27 January 2010

Metre: 6.6.6.6.D.

Suggested Tune: O MENTES PERFIDAS

Author's Note: Another text written for a Christmas card.

O MENTES PERFIDAS

Melody from Piae Cantiones, 1582
Arranged Nicholas Williams (1959–)

The silent night comes down and all seems safe and calm; his loving mother keeps her new-born son from harm. She holds him very close, drawn by his quietness, and lays him down to rest, awed by his helplessness.

Arrangement © Copyright 2011 Stainer & Bell Ltd

80 Our God is deepest mystery

Our God is deepest mystery,
beyond the farthest stars,
our God can never be described
by any words of ours;
and yet our God is very close,
the closest love can be,
a perfect Father whose great love
enfolds us tenderly.

God's deepest love has been made known,
displayed in helplessness,
where Jesus suffered on the cross,
and died in deep distress;
but now he comes, our Servant Lord,
forever glorified,
befriending and supporting us,
the brother at our side.

God's holy Spirit wraps us round
with deepest tenderness,
and like the kindest mother shares
our gladness and distress.
She comforts us and gives us strength
to grow up lovingly,
God's own dear children full of joy,
as we were born to be.

So, Love's eternal Trinity,
past all our words can say,
reveals a magnitude of love,
no power can take away;
which suffers people's pain and grief,
endures earth's agony,
and yearns to give us peace and joy
in Love's great family.

© Copyright 2009 Stainer & Bell Ltd

Written 22 October 2009

Metre: CMD

Suggested Tune: COE FEN

Author's Note: I saw, on television, a fourteen-year-old boy from a wealthy family, distressed in the presence of terminally ill children. He was asking, 'If there is a God, why are things like this allowed to happen?' A profound question, indeed. But it arises out of the notion that *Almighty God* has direct control of everything that happens in the world. I think that the worst thing we can do for our children is to bring them up with the idea of a super-strong God who can do anything. This started out as a hymn text for children, but ... well, I know that, as a child, I sang things not quite within my grasp, but learned from them. Why do we think that children are so simple?

81 Feel the wind blowing

Feel the wind blowing,
where does it come from?
Feel the wind blowing,
where does it go?
See the trees bending,
see the leaves flying,
see the waves crashing;
feel the wind blow.

Sit in the sunshine,
feel the breeze blowing,
gently refreshing
in summer's heat.
Leaves softly stirring,
bumble bees humming,
all the birds singing,
make peace complete.

God's Holy Spirit,
where do you come from?
God's Holy Spirit,
where do you go?
Forceful or gentle,
you come to claim us,
challenge and change us,
more than we know.

God's Holy Spirit,
where do we come from?
Where are we going?
How can we say?
Make us God's servants,
give us Love's freedom.
Following Jesus,
we know the way!

© Copyright 2010 Stainer & Bell Ltd

Written 19 May 2010

Metre: 5.5.5.4.D.

Suggested Tune: BUNESSAN

Author's Note: A Pentecost hymn for all-age worship.

82   When we are happy, when we are sad

When we are happy, when we are sad,
when we are good or when we are bad,
when we are healthy, when we are ill,
Jesus is here with the love of God:
Jesus who loves us and always will,
Jesus is here with the love of God.

When people suffer in pain and cry,
with all their neighbours passing them by,
when nobody seems to hear their prayers,
Jesus is there with the love of God:
Jesus who loves them and always cares,
Jesus is there with the love of God.

Jesus himself has borne pain and loss,
helpless and suffering on the cross,
crying to God in desperate prayer:
Jesus, who came with the love of God,
knowing such sadness and such despair,
Jesus, who came with the love of God.

God's love in Jesus is always near,
comforting grief and conquering fear:
God's love that Jesus calls us to share,
sending us out with the love of God,
to share with others God's loving care:
sending us out with the love of God.

© Copyright 2010 Stainer & Bell Ltd

Written 9 November 2010

Metre: 9 9.9.9.9.9.

Suggested Tune: STEPPING STONES

Author's Note: I have been quite disturbed by some of the simplistic hymns/songs for children, especially those which seem to me to be theologically, philosophically and scientifically untrue. I decided that I must try and produce some more serious texts for worship when children are present: believing, as I do, that children do not need simplistic language – they are capable of more understanding than some of us seem to think. I realise that this is not an easy text!

STEPPING STONES

Tony Davies (1945–)

When we are hap-py, when we are sad, when we are good or when we are bad, when we are health-y, when we are ill, Jesus is here with the love of God: Jesus who loves us and al-ways will, Jesus is here with the love of God.

© Copyright 2011 Stainer & Bell Ltd

83 Father, you love us

Father, you love us
most perfectly for ever;
your love overflows eternity.
You fill time and space
and in every place
you are there in love to set us free.

Jesus, our brother,
you laid your life down for us,
showing how true love is meant to be.
So let us, like you,
prove God's love is true:
living now to set each other free.

Spirit, empower us
to love and serve each other;
drive away all bitterness and strife.
Come and make us see
how love sets us free:
sharing peace, enriching our whole life.

Trinity, teach us
your perfect way of loving:
bound together, yet for ever free.
Keep us every day
bound on love's sure way,
till we share love's freedom endlessly!

© Copyright 2010 Stainer & Bell Ltd

Written June 2010

Metre: 5.7.9.5 5.9.

Suggested Tune: FATHER, WE LOVE YOU

Author's Note: The theme of worship was the persistent liberating love of God which was lived out by Jesus and which, because of our disunity, is not yet worked out by the Church in the world. There needs to be constant repentance and prayer if hope in 'love's sure way' is to be kept alive.

84 God, in Christ, your mighty Spirit

For Susan Durber and Westminster College

God, in Christ, your mighty Spirit
gave apostles their good news:
whose great mission we inherit,
whose transforming faith we choose.
Still your Spirit will empower us:
we will be apostles too
and, like those who went before us,
live to prove the Gospel true.

Give us scholarship for teaching,
wit and wisdom, patience, prayer.
Keep us eager, keep us learning,
give us more and more to share:
more of faith's courageous vision,
more of hope's expectancy,
crowned with love's eternal passion,
endless creativity.

By your Spirit's inspiration,
caught in stirring words and art,
kindle faith's imagination,
light up every mind and heart.
Give us, as we look and listen,
openness to see and hear
truth to change our life's direction,
love to heal earth's grief and fear.

Teaching, sharing, always learning,
God, we ask for no reward
but the privilege of being
servants with our Servant Lord.
As we journey on together,
let our faith and hope increase,
trusting love beyond all measure,
serving justice, truth and peace.

© Copyright 2011 Stainer & Bell Ltd

Written 18 January 2011

Metre: 8.7.8.7.D.

Suggested Tune: HYFRYDOL

Author's Note: Westminster College, Cambridge was working to broaden its influence in the United Reformed Church, so that it would not simply be training ministers, but encouraging everyone to go on learning and reflecting, so as to grow and flourish in faith. There was also to be an emphasis on faith and the arts, not simply on theology and book-learning. This text was written by request.

85 Handed over, dressed in purple

Handed over, dressed in purple,
with a cruel crown of thorns
thrust hard down around his temples,
Jesus was derided, scorned.
God, this mocked and helpless victim
was your own most precious Son;
made a fool, he was your wisdom,
and the cross became his throne.
Here is cause for glad thanksgiving!
Though it seemed that grief had won,
now we praise with joy and singing
God's crucified triumphant Son.

If, with him, we are made nothing,
nothingness will be our pride;
there's no greater cause for boasting,
than our love for Christ who died.
Power is vanquished by his weakness,
hatred conquered by his love,
death outdone where he is helpless.
This is what we live to prove!
Chorus

© Copyright 2011 Stainer & Bell Ltd

Written 13 January 2011

Metre: 8.7.8.7.D. and Chorus 8.7.8.7.

Suggested Tune: ESTUARY

Author's Note: The crucifixion of Jesus, as all crucifixions, burnings at the stake and other tortures, for political or religious reasons, was a terrible and cruel thing! It seemed for him like the end of everything, and yet faith sees God's glory and wisdom in it. And that glory and wisdom have gone on being worked out in all those who have been persecuted or martyred in the cause of justice and peace, whatever their faith or none. Holy Love is working out its purpose.

ESTUARY *Tony Davies (1945–)*

Handed over, dressed in purple, with a cruel crown of thorns
thrust hard down around his temples, Jesus was derided, scorned.
God, this mocked and helpless victim was your own most precious Son;
made a fool, he was your wisdom, and the cross became his throne.
Here is cause for glad thanksgiving! Though it seemed that grief had won,
now we praise with joy and singing God's crucified triumphant Son.

© Copyright 2011 Stainer & Bell Ltd

86 All glory, praise and honour

All glory, praise and honour,
Jesus, our Servant King,
to whom the lips of children
still make hosannas ring.
You are the dazzling servant,
the great and mighty One;
the humble king we worship
as God's own glorious Son.

We join our joyful praises,
to those who met you then,
when you rode on a donkey,
down to Jerusalem.
With waving palms they met you
and spread them on your way;
we join in their hosannas
and greet you here today!

We come, Lord, with thanksgiving,
to travel on with you,
so give us perseverance
to see the journey through.
Let prayer and praises flourish,
and give us faith to share
proof of your love and goodness,
for ever, everywhere.

© Copyright 2011 Stainer & Bell Ltd

Written 18 February 2011

Metre: 7.6.7.6.D.

Suggested Tune: ST THEODULPH

Author's Note: J. M. Neale translated Theodulf of Orleans's Latin hymn as 'All glory, laud and honour', still popular for Palm Sunday. This is not a translation but a new text, with acknowledgement to Neale and Theodulf for the inspiration.

87 Lord, as we follow you

Lord, as we follow you,
keep us for ever true
to your own ministry of love and healing.
Through all our pain and fear,
remain for ever near,
to conquer in us every frightened feeling.

Jesus, you lead the way
and we, from day to day,
are called to trust in you and bravely follow.
And yet we must confess
the faith that we profess
is far too often feeble, false and hollow.

And yet your love remains,
your pity still sustains
our faltering hearts, and by your inspiration,
uplifted, we shall share
in joyful praise and prayer,
and greet your endless love with jubilation!

So let us come to be
your witnesses, set free
to read each neighbour into love's great story;
redeem our doubts and fears
and lead us through the years,
to serve the world and praise your deathless glory.

© Copyright 2011 Stainer & Bell Ltd

Written 18 February 2011

Metre: 6 6.11.D.

Suggested Tune: DOWN AMPNEY

Author's Note: A confessional hymn about following Jesus into the world, in spite of all our weaknesses and failings.

88   Lord Jesus, we have heard

Lord Jesus, we have heard
how humbly once you came;
not as a conquering king,
not seeking praise or fame;
you rode down to Jerusalem
and there, for love's sake, risking all
you challenged people with God's call.

Lord Jesus, let us still
respond to you today,
and follow where you lead,
however hard the way.
Through disillusion, danger, doubt,
still challenge us to hear God's call
and go, for love's sake, risking all.

If we are gripped by fear,
dragged down by grief or pain,
if, anxious or depressed,
we bitterly complain,
forgive us and restore our faith;
still challenge us to hear God's call
and go, for love's sake, risking all.

When we have followed you,
our trusted guide and friend,
when we have loved and served,
we'll praise you at the end:
so full of thankfulness and joy,
delighted that we heard God's call
and came, for love's sake, risking all.

© Copyright 2011 Stainer & Bell Ltd

19 February 2011

Metre: 6.6.6.6.8.8 8.

Suggested Tune: RHOSYMEDRE

Author's Note: This was written for Palm Sunday, the idea behind it being that Jesus riding down to Jerusalem was 'risking all ...' and praying, in effect, that we who metaphorically follow him into Jerusalem might follow him all the way.

89   The welcome birth of every girl and boy

The welcome birth of every girl and boy
should bind their parents' lives with ties of joy.
Love's innocence, a small and tender flame,
shines out and stakes its overriding claim.

Helplessness reigns and in an infant's cries,
innocence schools the wisdom of the wise;
and infancy's relentless, guileless art,
claims the complete devotion of the heart.

But when revenge and war demand their price
and children's lives are made the sacrifice,
if we condone hate's justifying lie
it would be better we ourselves should die.

So, as we celebrate this infant's birth,
and think of Christ, once helpless on this earth,
we bring our child to him in confidence,
and dare to meet our own first innocence.

Here we naïvely yearn that rage will end
and mercy, gentleness and peace descend,
like some far journeying and wounded dove,
to plead and prove the power of powerless love.

© Copyright 2011 Stainer & Bell Ltd

Written 4 March 2011

Metre: 10 10.10 10.

Suggested Tunes: CHILTON FOLIAT and FFIGYSBREN

Author's Note: This was originally written on 3 January 2004 (No. 12) and used for a Christmas card in 2005, which had on it the stylised image of a dove in flight. It was revised in this form for a service of Infant Baptism. It might also be used for an Infant Dedication or Blessing. Verse 3 might seem a bit strong for such a service: it could be excluded, but some parents might find it appropriate.

Index of First Lines and Titles

First lines of choruses are shown in *italics*;
titles are shown in UPPER CASE

A HYMN AFTER SUDDEN DEATH   31
A HYMN FOR JOHN CALVIN AFTER 500 YEARS   69
All glory, praise and honour   86
Any child born to loving parents might   12
As Christ hangs crucified   18
Be with us, Servant Lord   56
Christ, challenge us to understand   22
Christ, from eternity   13
Christ, hold us in your loving arms   52
Christ, nations, hard at war   21
Claim all our lives and send us out to share   39
Columba, long ago in Ireland   63
Dancing Holy Trinity   9
Don't let love fail, Lord   78
Don't tell me your sorrows, I can't share your pain   67
Eternal God, whose love is ever true   31
Eternal God, you live and move   62
Eternal Spirit, once you drove   10
Father, you love us   83
Feel the wind blowing   81
Forgive us, God, each crass attempt   7
Give us, great Christ, out of your majesty   51
God, destroy the bigotry   11
God, give us grace to rise above   42
God, in Christ, your mighty Spirit   84
God, our Creator, Source of truth and justice   38
God, save from cruel persecution   26
God, speak to us in all who meet us   17
God, you see your pleas for justice   57
GOOD FRIDAY LEADS TO HOLY SATURDAY   37
Great crucified and risen Lord   4
Great God of love, you know us through and through   64
Great God of love, you share your children's pain   74
Great God of Moses, so tenderly yearning   71
Great Holy Spirit, gentle injured dove   47
Handed over, dressed in purple   85
Help us, Jesus, to be like you   76
Here, God is present with us   29
Here, in this world of sadness   28
Here is cause for glad thanksgiving!   85

His terrified disciples   35
Holy Spirit, gentle dove   39
How blessed are those, our loving God   48
In music we express delight   66
It is too late to pray   43
Jesus, God's precious child on earth   50
Jesus, our friend, you are always near   27
Jesus, uniquely bodied in each neighbour   15
Jesus, whose wounding wins the world   45
John the Baptist told King Herod   5
Let's count the stars and if we ever finish   68
Let's count the stars, perhaps when we have finished   68
Look! I'm so light   67
Lord, as we follow you   87
Lord Jesus, we have heard   88
Lord, whose wealth is all around us   25
Loud, from the cross, a shout is heard   14
LOVE SONG   1
Love that made us, Love that saved us   49
Loving God, like a father or mother   49
Loving God, your radiant sunlight   59
Make us your prophets, Lord   53
Man on a donkey, come to town   55
Mary, friend of Jesus, Mary Magdalen   58
Mary gave birth to her child   77
My child sleeps quietly   2
Our God is deepest mystery   80
Perfect sunlit dawning   60
Saint David was dying   70
See where the birds   30
So, God, keep us serving   70
Speak to us, Christ, in strangers   16
Spirit, coming in the splendour   65
Stay here where nails are driven   40
Suffering servant   23
Tell all the world about it   35
The baby sleeps in mother-love's strong arms   46
The bush burns unconsumed   44
The darkest day was past   24
The silent night comes down   79
The true Church is found where God's purpose is sovereign   69
The voice that makes the world go dark   54
The welcome birth of every girl and boy   89
There is a day when faith discerns   37
There is no limit, God   19

There was a day   20
They ran and ran, so full of joy   72
This is our confidence: in Christ love died for us   8
This world so full of hatred needs   41
Though grief and pain, persisting   28
Two people walked their weary way   36
We are not as loving as we ought to be   76
We bring our thanks, our gracious God   75
We have not seen you with wounded hands   34
We praise your dying love   3
We speak so many words   73
What ails my child   1
When helpless infants suffer pain   33
When no words can suffice   6
When we are happy, when we are sad   82
When your children are in distress   78
With Jesus as our mirror   32
Yes, Mary, we have greeted   61
You will not fail us, great God our Creator   8

Index of Tunes

Tunes printed in this anthology are marked ★

ABBOT'S LEIGH	8.7.8.7.D.	59
AFORO-KWABI★	8.8.8.8.8.8.	66
AURELIA	7.6.7.6.D.	32
BABYLON★	13.13.7.7.13.	5
BEYOND ALL WORDS★	6.6.6.6.D.	6
BLACKBIRD LEYS	10.10.10.10.	64
BRESLAU	LM	14, 42, 55
BUNESSAN	5.5.5.4.D.	81
CHARTRES	7.7.7.7.7.6.7.6.	61
CHILTON FOLIAT	10.10.10.10.	89
CHRISTUS DER IST MEIN LEBEN	7.6.7.6.	16
CLIFF TOWN	6.4.6.4.D.	18
COE FEN	CMD	80
COLLIERY GREEN★	6.6.6.6.D.	2
CORROUR BOTHY	6.6.8.4.	13
DISTANT HILLS★	4.6.4.6.D.	30
DON'T LET LOVE FAIL, LORD★	LMD and Chorus 5.8.	78
DOWN AMPNEY	6.6.11.D.	53, 87
DUNDRENNAN	SM	3, 56
EBENEZER	8.7.8.7.D.	57
EDMONDSHAM	7.6.7.6.	29
EISENACH	LM	10, 52
ELLERS	10.10.10.10.	31
EPIPHANY HYMN	11.10.11.10.	71
ESTUARY★	8.7.8.7.D. and Chorus 8.7.8.7.	85
EVENTIDE (Monk)	10.10.10.10.	31
FAITHFULNESS	11.10.11.10. and Chorus 12.10.11.10.	8
FATHER, WE LOVE YOU	5.7.9.5.5.9.	83
FFIGYSBREN	10.10.10.10.	89
FRANCONIA	SM	44
FULDA	LM	52
GO TELL IT ON THE MOUNTAIN	7.6.7.6. and Chorus 7.9.7.6.	28, 35
GREAT HOLY SPIRIT, GENTLE INJURED DOVE★	10.4.4.10.8.8.	47
GRIEF★	4.4.4.4.4.6.6.	20
HARINGTON	CM	22
HAWKHURST	LM	4
HERONGATE	LM	7, 33
HOLY SPIRIT, GENTLE DOVE★	10.10.8.8. and Chorus 7.7.9.8.9.8.	39
HYFRYDOL	8.7.8.7.D.	84

ICH HALTE TREULICH STILL	SMD	24
INTERCESSOR	11.10.11.10.	15
KINGSFOLD	CMD	36, 50, 75
LAWES PSALM 47	6.6.6.6.8.8.	73
LES COMMANDEMENS DE DIEU	9.8.9.8.	17, 26
LOVE UNKNOWN	6.6.6.6.8.8.	43
LOVELY JOAN	9.8.9.8.	27
MAGDA	10.10.10.10.	12, 51
MELITA	8.8.8.8.8.8.	62
NOËL NOUVELET	11.11.11.11.	58
O MENTES PERFIDAS★	6.6.6.6.D.	79
O WALY WALY	LM	54
O WALY WALY	9.8.9.8.	27, 34
ODE TO JOY	8.7.8.7.D.	65
OLWEN	6.6.8.6.6.8.D. and Chorus 6.6.8.D.	70
OVERCHURCH★	11.11.11.11. and Chorus 8.7.8.9.	76
PARSLEY HAY★	7.5.7.5.7.5.7.6.	9
QUEM PASTORES	8.8.8.7.	25
RHOSYMEDRE	6.6.6.6.8.8.8.	88
RUTH (Smith)	6.5.6.5.D.	60
SCOTFORTH★	4.4.4.6.D.	1
SEARCHING FOR LAMBS	9.8.9.8.	34
SERVANT LORD★	5.4.5.6.5.4.6.8.	23
SHELTERED DALE	8.6.8.6.8.6.	72
SHEPHERDS' FIELD★	7.7.7.7.D. and Chorus 7.7.6.5.10.	77
SHRUB END	7.6.7.6.	40
SING HOSANNA	10.8.10.9. and Chorus 8.9.8.7.	49
SO LIGHT★	11.11.11.11. and Chorus 4.5.6.5.	67
SOM STRANDEN	11.10.11.10.11.10.	38, 68
SOUTHWELL	SM	21
SPIRITUS VITAE	9.8.9.8.	17, 26
ST CATHERINE'S COURT	12.11.12.11.	69
ST THEODULPH	7.6.7.6.D.	86
STEPPING STONES★	9.9.9.9.9.9.	82
THE BABY SLEEPS IN MOTHER-LOVE'S STRONG ARMS★	10.10.10.	46
THIRD MODE MELODY	CMD	41, 50
TON-Y-BOTEL	8.7.8.7.D.	57
TRURO	LM	45
TUNE FOR MARY	7.6.7.6.D.	11
VALIANT HEARTS	10.10.10.10.	74
WAREHAM	LM	37
WINCHESTER NEW	LM	48
WINDERMERE	SM	19
YE BANKS AND BRAES	9.8.9.8.8.8.8.8.	63

Subject Index

God
Creator   38
Incarnate   19, 62
Love   19, 49, 68, 83
Transcendent and unknown   68, 73, 80
Trinity   9, 11, 29, 49, 64, 80

Jesus Christ
Birth   1, 2, 12, 46, 61, 77, 79
Friendship   27
Helplessness   12, 14, 22, 24, 51, 55, 77, 79, 85, 89
His presence   82
Holy Saturday   20, 37
Incarnation   10, 13, 62
Love   22, 78, 82, 83
Palm Sunday   55, 86, 88
Passion   3, 8, 13, 14, 18, 19, 22, 37, 40, 42, 45, 73, 77, 84, 85
Resurrected   8, 24, 34, 35, 36, 58, 60, 72
Sacrifice and triumph   13

The Holy Spirit
Claiming and inspiring   39
Flouted   47
In creation   65
Pentecost   81
With Christ   10

The Church and its worship
Confession   7, 11, 23, 42, 43, 45, 47, 57, 67
Creativity   30
Eucharist/Holy Communion   50
Funeral   3, 31, 48
Healing and wholeness   4, 29
Infant Baptism/blessing/dedication   89
Music   66
Ordination   56, 71
Praise   30, 66, 85, 86
Thanks   75, 85
The Church   23, 69, 75

Christian life and witness
Bereavement   3, 31, 48
Commitment   8, 23, 38, 53, 87, 88
Compassion   41
Confident assurance   8
Conservation   65
Fellowship   75
Grief   6, 31, 33, 66
Eternal life   48
Joy   3, 6, 8, 9, 28, 30, 35, 39, 60, 66, 72
Justice and Peace   11, 21, 26, 42, 43, 57, 59, 61, 63
Love   4, 22, 67, 76, 83
Neighbours   15, 17, 32, 76
Reconciliation and Unity   11, 64
Remembrance   21, 54, 74
Self-sacrifice   22
Service   4, 23, 41, 84
Slavery   57
Strangers   16, 17
Suffering   78
The Church   38, 59, 69
Trust   25, 52
Unity/Week of Prayer   69
Witness/Mission   8, 22, 23, 24, 35, 44, 45, 51, 52, 53, 56, 59, 72, 83, 84, 85, 87

Bible, and other, characters and stories
Cleopas   36
John Calvin   69
Mary, mother of Jesus   1, 2, 46, 61, 77, 79
Mary Magdalen   58
Moses   44, 71
Saint Columba   63
St David   70
Thomas   34
Samaritan Woman   71

Acknowledgements

The extracts from Vernon Watkins's poems *Deposition, On the Painting by Ceri Richards* (pages v, 20 and 46), *Sonnet, To Certain Ancient Anonymous Poets* (page 50) and *The Childhood of Hölderlin* (page 50) are taken from *The Collected Poems of Vernon Watkins*, published by Golgonooza Press, 1986. Used by permission of Mrs Gwen Watkins.

The extract on page vi from Brian Wren's hymn 'Great God, your love has called us here' is © 1975, 1995 Stainer & Bell Ltd.

The extract on page viii from *Readings in St John's Gospel, Second Series* by William Temple (Macmillan, 1940) is reproduced with permission of Palgrave Macmillan.

The extract on page ix from the sonnet *Never Understood* by Alan Gaunt is taken from *The Space Between* (Songster, 2009) and is used by permission of the author.

Extracts from the poems *Late and Deep* (page 17), *Wan-voiced* (page 55) and *14 Poems from Breathturn* (pages viii and 87) are taken from *Selected Poems and Prose of Paul Celan* by Paul Celan, translated by John Felstiner. Copyright © 2001 by John Felstiner. Used by permission of W. W. Norton & Company, Inc.

The extract from the poem *Late and Deep* (page 17) is translated from the original German poem *Spät und tief* by Paul Celan, from his collection *Mohn und Gedächtnis*, © 1952, Deutsche Verlags-Anstalt, München, in der Verlagsgruppe Random House GmbH. Used by permission.

The extract from the poem beginning *Wan-voiced* (page 55) is translated from the original German poem beginning *Fahlstimmig* by Paul Celan, from his collection *Lichtzwang*, © 1970 Suhrkamp Verlag GmbH & Co. KG. Used by permission.

The extract from *14 Poems from Breathturn* (pages viii and 87) is translated from the original German collection *Atemwende* by Paul Celan, © 1967 Suhrkamp Verlag GmbH & Co. KG. Used by permission.

Extracts from the poems *Death as Perfection* (page 19), *God's Love* (page 19), *God's Sacrament* (page 20), *God's Footfall* (page 20), *God's One Body* (page 21), *Christ's Lifted Arms* (page 24) and *Flesh Transfigured* (page 24) are all taken from Stella Aldwinckle's collection *Christ's Shadow in Plato's Cave*, published by The Amate Press, Oxford, 1990. Copyright holder untraced.

Extracts from *A Letter to Pablo Antonio Cuadra Concerning Giants* by Thomas Merton (pages 22 and 23) are taken from *The Collected Poems of Thomas Merton*, copyright © 1963 by The Abbey of Gesthemani. Reprinted by permission of New Directions Publishing Corp.

The extracts on pages 25, 26 and 29 from *Between Cross and Resurrection: A Theology of Holy Saturday* by Alan E. Lewis, and the extract on page 83 from *The Theology of John Calvin* by Karl Barth, translated by Geoffrey W. Bromiley, are used by permission of Wm B Eerdmans Publishing Company.

The extract on page 41 from the *Odes of Solomon* 13 is taken from *The Odes and Psalms of Solomon* by J. R. Harris and A. Mingana, published by Manchester University Press and Longmans, Green, 1916–1920. Copyright holder untraced.

The Scripture quotations on pages 43 and 82 are taken from the New Revised Standard Version Bible, © copyright 1989, Division of Christian Education of the National Council of the Churches of Christ in the United States of America. Used by permission. All rights reserved.

The extract on page 50 from *Hopeful Imagination: Prophetic Voices in Exile* by Walter Brueggemann is used by permission of Augsburg Fortress Publishers.

The quotation on page 55 from the Reverend James Gordon Gilkey's letter printed in *The New York Times* on 7 June 1944 is used by permission of Professor Peter B. Gilkey.

The extracts on page 77 from Martin Palmer's book *Living Christianity* are used by permission of the author.

The extracts on page 86 from Margaret Cropper's poem *A Fragment* are taken from *Selected Poems* by Margaret Cropper, published in 1958 by Titus Wilson and Son Ltd. Used by permission of The Margaret Cropper Trust.